OUT

"All you need is this guide to map your way to various factory outlets all over the South."

—*Living in South Carolina*

"Of interest to anyone trying to find Southern outlets."

—*Tennessee Librarian*

"Shopping hounds will find good reading in this paperback guide."

—*Baton Rouge Magazine*

OUTLET GUIDE:
South

Alabama, Arkansas, Florida, Georgia,
Kentucky, Louisiana, Mississippi, North Carolina,
South Carolina, and Tennessee

Third Edition

by A. Miser and A. Pennypincher

A Voyager Book

The Globe Pequot Press

Old Saybrook, Connecticut

Library of Congress Cataloging-in-Publication Data

Miser, A.
    Outlet guide: South : Alabama, Arkansas, Florida, Georgia, Kentucky, Louisiana, Mississippi, North Carolina, South Carolina, and Tennessee / by A. Miser and A. Pennypincher. — 3rd ed.
        p. cm.
    Rev. ed. of: Factory outlet guide to the South. 2nd ed. 1992.
    "A Voyager book."—t.p.
    Includes indexes.
    ISBN 1-56440-387-4
    1. Outlet stores—Southern States—Directories. I. Pennypincher, A. II. Miser, A. Factory outlet guide to the South. III. Title.
HF5429.4.A2M57 1994
381'.15'02575—dc20   93-47496
                                                         CIP

Manufactured in the United States of America
Third Edition/First Printing

Contents

Contents

Introduction

"Outlet Shopping Is Big Business With 300 Centers and $9 Billion in Sales," proclaimed the headline of a recent Associated Press article. This claim is especially true in the American South. Textiles have always been synonymous with the South, and usually, where there were textiles . . . there were factory outlets. From their first spartan existence, factory outlets have become big business, largely due to the fact that they are now carefully planned and located. There are factory outlet consultants who work with cities to bring this shopping phenomenon to fruition. (For information on consulting, contact Factory Outlet Consultants, Headquarters Office, Carleton Bob Meyers, President, 5641 Burke Centre Parkway, Suite 220, Burke, Virginia 22015; 703–250–5166. Or, if you are interested in information on how you can become an outlet owner yourself, contact *Value Retail News,* 800–669–1020. Mainly this book is geared toward shoppers.)

Today, factory outlets in the South are highly sophisticated in both appearance and merchandise. Although they do offer some defective merchandise (which is marked), the discerning shopper will also find considerable bargains in overruns (too many of a style manufactured to meet demand) and dated goods. Do not assume that factory outlets have only low-quality or undesirable merchandise; many prestigious manufacturers are involved with this marketing approach, and as you browse through this book, you will see innumerable well-known brand names. Alert manufacturers have sensed the latent potential in this approach and learned to capitalize on it.

Although the South is dotted with factory outlets in single units, malls and cluster developments are gaining popularity. Often such malls can be found in small towns, off the beaten path, since this business venture greatly increases the tax base of a city (otherwise, those cities might have been in danger of vanishing, as they watched their agricultural base slip away with the farm crisis). Most outlet mall complexes, however, will be found along popular interstates.

And what can you expect in your constant battle against inflation? When you shop at factory outlets, you can shop at "sale" prices throughout the year. It is realistic to say that in the course of a year you could save 50 percent of your budgeted dollars by shopping at factory stores. Or on the other side of the coin, you could spend your budget but buy twice as much.

Factory outlet malls generally offer easy parking and a diversity of top-quality stores carrying virtually everything from toys to shoes, at savings of 25 to 70 percent. Refer to the Profiles in Savings section of this book for special notes or ask to be put on the outlet's mailing list, if it has one.

Individual outlets may not appear as cosmopolitan as the malls, but don't judge them on their outward appearance. Outlets of all kinds offer large discounts based on low overhead, and as one friend once reminded us, "One person's 'junque' is another person's treasure."

Planning Your Shopping Trip

The abundance of factory outlet complexes has forced us to become highly organized in planning a shopping trip. Here are our suggestions for a productive shopping expedition to factory outlets.

Take a loose-leaf notebook and divide it into sections. One section should be for each person for whom you buy clothing or anything else during the course of the year; jot down sizes, needs, color preferences, and desires. Another section should be for your home on a room-by-room basis; keep additional pages for other categories as the need arises. With such pertinent information on hand, you can go shopping with confidence.

When you're clothes shopping for adults at a factory outlet, you can afford to think in terms of "investment" clothing. Suits for men and women, as well as blazers, skirts, and pants, fall into this category. An expensive suit should last for years; for it to do so requires that you carefully study the styling, quality, and tailoring details. You can also afford to supplement your basic wardrobe with less expensive items that reflect the whims of fashion. A blouse in the current "in" shades can be discarded in another season when fashion dictates a new shade; you won't feel so wasteful if that blouse cost only a few dollars at the factory outlet. But remember, planning is the key here—know what you actually need for your wardrobe before you go. Impulse buying of colors, styles, and fabrics that will not fit in or are never worn does not yield a good buy, no matter how low the price.

It is unrealistic to expect most teenagers and growing children to think in terms of investment clothing. Young people are often too involved in the mainstream of current trends and fashions—not to mention the fact that they can grow inches each year. The basic concept of investment shopping, however, needs to be taught in children's formative years. Teenagers begin to show their independence through their clothing; therefore, wise parents will take the child with them to ensure not only that the garment fits but that it will be worn once it's purchased. (Outlets vary in their return policies, a point to keep in mind when shopping without the person involved.) Then you can be glad for the low prices of the factory outlets that enable you to indulge your child with fads in fashion. (Hint: You may want to ask about the returns policy and jot it down on the back of your receipt.)

The notebook section on your home should contain such essential information as window sizes, color schemes, fabric samples, and furniture needs. It would be a shame to have to pass up the "ultimate bargain" just because you didn't have the proper measurements. (Adding color photos of room layouts would also give you a current "inventory" should fire or theft occur since insurance companies require proof of such a claim.)

It is also a good idea to dedicate a separate section of your notebook to gift buying for the special people in your life. Month by month, determine all your gift-giving needs and you'll find endless possibilities for low-cost gifts that project a first-class image. (By adding pocket folders to your notebook, you can store greeting cards purchased on the same gift-buying trip; by doing so, when the "special event" arises you'll be totally prepared.)

Once your notebook is complete, browse through local establishments to get a feel for retail pricing, current styles, and color combinations. (You may want to make special pricing notations in the margins of your book to get a true comparison of outlet "deals.") Then you'll be ready to begin serious shopping.

One final thought: Consider including a shopping trip during a vacation. You may find that your savings on a major buying trip, such as one undertaken before the opening of school, will help you pay for your vacation. (Don't ever lose sight, though, of your budget, since outlets offer the very best in tempting purchases.) Because this book is dedicated to the budget conscious and we know that vacations can also be expensive, we recommend planning to help with that budget, too. Taking this aspect into consideration, we have included a list of state contacts for you to write to when planning a vacation. These offices can help you in selecting a bed-and-breakfast establishment, for instance, instead of paying for an expensive motel or renting a costly condominium. When writing these sources, be sure to ask for updated information on outlets in the area you plan to visit. (The industry is growing so fast that there is no way to keep up with all of them.) Moreover, be aware that some cities—like Boaz, Alabama; Dalton, Georgia; and Hickory, North Carolina—are almost entirely devoted to outlet shopping. The more you save on your vacation, the more you have to spend at outlets.

State Tourism Information

Alabama
Bureau of Tourism & Travel
401 Adams Avenue
Montgomery, AL 36104–4616
(205) 242–4169

Arkansas
Tourism Division
Division of Parks & Tourism
One Capitol Mall
Little Rock, AR 72201–1014
(501) 682–7777

Florida
Division of Tourism, Department of Commerce
505 Collins Building
107 West Gaines Street
Tallahassee, FL 32399–6549
(904) 487–1462

Georgia
Tourist Division, Department of Industry & Trade
285 Peachtree Center Avenue, N.E.
Marquis Tower #2, Suite 1000
Atlanta, GA 30303–1230
(404) 656–3553

Kentucky
Department of Travel Development
500 Mero St., Suite 2200
Frankfort, KY 40601–1968
(502) 564–4930

Louisiana
Office of Tourism
900 Riverside Street
Baton Rouge, LA 70802–5236
(504) 342–8119

Mississippi
Tourism Division
550 High Street, Suite 1200
Jackson, MS 39201–1113
(601) 359–3297

North Carolina
Travel and Tourism Divison
430 North Salisbury Street
Raleigh, NC 27611
(919) 733–4171

South Carolina
Division of Tourism (Parks, Recreation & Tourism)
1205 Pendleton Street
Columbia, SC 29201–3731
(803) 734–0135

Tennessee
Department of Tourist Development
320 Sixth Avenue, N.
Nashville, TN 37243–3170
(615) 741–2159

Using This Book

To simplify the use of this book, we have divided it into several sections:

1. Profiles in Savings, to reduce duplication of material, includes generic information on the outlets listed in this book. The name of one company's outlets may vary slightly from one location to another; therefore, we have listed these name variations in this section whenever we think you might be confused.

2. Maps are included prior to each individual state section to assist you in locating the cities where outlets can be found.

3. State sections are designed with cities listed in alphabetical order. Also included are addresses and phone numbers as well as information on hours of operation, food establishments located nearby, unique qualities about the outlet mall, financial requirements, whether bus tours are welcome, and any other notes or attractions about the geographic area of the outlet mall. By federal law, all outlets that cater to the public must be handicapped-accessible.

4. Specialized indexes are included at the end of the book.

In compiling the data for this book, we have made every attempt to provide accurate information. But outlets do go out of business; they do sometimes close for vacation; they do change hours—and they even move. There is no way we can control or predict the ebb and flow of commercial endeavors. Do not, then, go any great distance without first checking to see whether things have changed since this book was written. Likewise, don't assume that a particular outlet is located in an outlet center just because a similar center has that outlet as an anchor establishment. Leasing arrangements vary from state to state.

If outlets are in an area affected by tourism—as are many of the towns in North and South Carolina and Florida—their hours may fluctuate in order to benefit from the influx of seasonal visitors; be prepared for such extensions or for reduction of hours in the off-season.

Many of the outlets accept credit cards; those that do not are so indicated in the listing. Accordingly, take along cash or your checkbook with at least two forms of identification, preferably at least one with a photograph.

If saving money is important to you, this guide can be extremely helpful. Look upon factory outlet shopping as a challenging game, with the winner being you (and your budget), and you'll certainly enjoy your savings adventure.

Finding New Manufacturers

No outlet owner may purchase inclusion in this book. Outlet inclusion is purely a personal decision on the part of the authors. In addition, *some outlets chose not to participate in the compilation of this book;* providing pertinent information was on a purely voluntary basis. You may, however, see outlets along the roadside while you are touring the southern states. Refer to the Profiles in Savings section of this book to see if a detour is worth your while.

Authors' visits to outlets are unannounced and anonymous so as to avoid special treatment or promotional influence. Future editions of this guide will allow for additions of new factory outlets. To have an outlet considered for inclusion, please address questions or comments to The Globe Pequot Press, P.O. Box 833, Old Saybrook, Connecticut 06475. All inquiries will be given careful consideration for future editions. References from readers of this volume will be greatly appreciated.

OUTLET GUIDE:
South

Profiles in Savings

A & K Gift
T-shirts, souvenirs, toys, and gifts from Florida at a discount.

Accessorize
Belts, hats, purses, and scarves at 30 percent off retail prices. Costume jewelry at 50 percent off retail prices.

Accessory Stop
Top off any outfit at 25 to 70 percent off regular retail prices. Pins, bracelets, scarves, belts, hair ornaments, necklaces, earrings, handbags, watches, designer jackets, and bridal accessories.

Acme Boot
Name-brand fashions at the best prices around to fit men, women, and children. Stock includes brands like Acme, Dingo, and Dan Post boots, as well as Minnetonka moccasins. Choose from authentic western boots to dress boots with exotic skins and leathers. Wrangler Western Wear and an assortment of name-brand hats are offered. Work boots are also included in the stock, which numbers more than five thousand. Accessories include western belt buckles and rattlesnake key chains. Expect savings from 40 to 60 percent off first-quality retail prices; discounts on seconds may reach 75 percent. Shipping available anywhere in the United States and Canada. Stock varies from store to store. Size ranges: infants' size 4 up to women's 10 and men's 13+. Returns: receipt required. No refunds or exchanges on worn merchandise. Layaway: 25 percent down, with a $3.00 nonrefundable fee. Eight-week payment period. Mail orders offered.

Adolfo II
Ladies' sportswear by Adolfo and Rafael, plus dresses by Donna Toran and DT II. Discounts vary by brand.

Adrienne Vittadini

Starting at savings of 40 percent and more. Select from the full assortment of current collections in sportswear, dresses, and accessories.

Aileen

First-quality, American-made women's sportswear at up to 70 percent off suggested retail prices every day. Missy, petite, and women's sizes. Manufacturer owned and operated. Best selections at beginning of seasons. Each location maintains a mailing list. Receipt required for all refunds. Nonsale merchandise refund or exchange within thirty days of purchase. Sale merchandise exchange only within thirty days of purchase. When using personal check for purchases, a ten-day waiting period is required before a refund is given.

Allan's Fashion Outlet

A one-price dress shop. All dresses are $24 (Leslie Tucks, Toni Todd, Melissa Lane, Lady Carole, Sears, and JCPenney, etc.); all sportswear, $12 (Sears, JCPenney, Remo, and Modular).

Allen Edmonds

Discounted men's and women's shoes; carries Allen Edmonds brand; men's sizes 5–16 AAAA–EEE, women's sizes 4–12 AAAA–C.

Alpine Festival of Arts & Crafts

Local and area artists and craftspersons show and sell their quality items at a discount price.

American Eagle Outfitters

Ladies' and men's clothing at 25 to 70 percent off regular retail prices.

American Tourister

From 25 to 70 percent off suggested retail prices on "gorilla tough" hard-side luggage, soft-side luggage, business cases, and sport bags. Travel accessories such as luggage carts. Sizes range from 16-inch totes to 60-inch overseas cases.

Amity

Quality leather goods, accessories, and travel items for men and women at savings from 25 to 75 percent off suggested retail. Factory owned and operated.

Amy Stoudt
First-quality fashions for the full-figured woman. Discounted 20 to 50 percent off manufacturer's retail price every day. Sizes 14W–32W.

Anne Klein
Direct factory outlet for Anne Klein & Company, Anne Klein II, and Anne Klein accessories including jewelry, perfume, watches, and handbags. Everyday savings up to 70 percent off suggested retail prices.

Anne's Dress Shop
Discounts vary on dresses, by manufacturer.

Ann's Diamond Center
Full-service jeweler offering a vast selection of diamonds, gold, pearls, stones, and watches, all at fantastic savings.

Arrow Factory Store
Save 30 to 70 percent off suggested retail prices on Arrow dress, sport, and knit shirts, sweaters, pants, ties, Gold Toe socks, and more.

Athlete's Foot
A sports buff will find savings of at least 30 percent. Savings vary by manufacturer.

Audrey Jones
Ladies' wear at 25 to 70 percent off regular retail prices.

Aunt Mary's Yarns
Crafts and needlework supplies at a discount.

Aureus
Active sportswear for men and women, 30 to 70 percent off suggested retail prices.

Avon Fashions
Women's and children's clothing at below retail cost. Women's sizes 3/4

to 18; Bright's Creek children's clothing from six months to sixteen years. Store will take Avon catalog orders.

Baby Guess
Manufacturer of designer, casual children's wear. Sizes 6 months to 6X/7. Substantial savings off suggested retail price.

Bag and Baggage
A luggage and handbag outlet featuring a complete selection of famous-name luggage, business cases, and handbags at 20 to 50 percent off suggested retail prices.

Bagmakers
Bags at 25 to 70 percent off regular retail prices.

Balloons Unlimited
Balloons, gifts, and specialty items at 30 to 60 percent savings.

Bally
Men's and women's shoes, leather jackets, briefcases, ties, belts, wallets, handbags, and other accessories, always 25 to 60 percent off.

B&G Leather Hut
Leather accessories at 25 to 70 percent off retail cost.

Banister Shoes (U.S. Shoe)
Forty major shoe brands. Women's and men's dress, casual, and athletic shoes. Save up to 50 percent every day. Brands include Adidas, Etonic, Bass, Reebok, Manistee, Surfsiders, Puma, Capezio, Candies, The Dancers, and Mushrooms.

Barbizon Lingerie
Carries only Barbizon sleepwear. All merchandise is first quality. Expect 25 to 70 percent off retail prices. Complete line of Myonne panties and Youthcraft bras and panty girdles. Daywear line is all Barbizon; the store usually has complete sizes, ranging from petite to 3X.

Barett Shoes
A new concept in women's fashion shoe stores. Women's designer and

famous-name brands at $13.88, $16.88, and $19.88. Everything a mall store has except high prices. Thousands of pairs. New styles arrive weekly. All the newest and most-wanted styles.

Barry Manufacturing Company

The latest in men's traditional and Italian-model clothing at wholesale prices, whereby the middleman is eliminated because the stock comes straight from the manufacturer. Savings of at least 50 to 70 percent off retail prices on thousands of garments. Popular hard- and soft-finish fabrics; natural and synthetic fibers; imported and domestic fabrics. Accessories, outerwear, and formalwear, too. Mailing list maintained by store. Sizes for everyone: regular 36–60; long 37–60; X-long 40–54; short 35–72; boys' sizes 12–20. Exchanges within thirty days with receipt on nonaltered clothing. Free ninety-day layaway with thirty-day payments.

Bass Apparel

Men's and women's casuals. Save up to 40 percent on famous brands.

Bass Shoes

Save 25 percent or more off the regular retail price on Weejuns, Bucs, Sunjuns sandals, and other classic footwear and accessories every day at the Bass Factory Outlet. You'll find full-grain leathers, rich fashion colors, and the attention to detail that's been a Bass hallmark for more than a hundred years.

Bath Shop

Accessories and necessities for the bath at 25 to 70 percent off regular retail prices.

Beacon Blanket Boutique

Beacon-brand blankets, spreads, infant products, and institutional blankets from the nation's largest manufacturer of blankets. The outlet also carries Fieldcrest, Cannon, and St. Mary's towels and Bibb sheets and comforters—a complete bed-and-bath shop offering both firsts and irregulars, at 30 to 60 percent savings.

Bealls

Famous brands of clothing and accessories for the entire family. New arrivals weekly. Closeouts and irregulars. Discounts vary. Big savings on first quality, too.

Belgian Rug Company

A large selection of beautiful Oriental-design rugs imported from Belgium . . . value priced.

Benetton

European styling in knits and bright colors for the young . . . and the young at heart. Children's clothing by Benetton (0–12). Menswear includes Benetton brands and others. Womenswear includes Benetton, Sisley, Armani, 012, and Veracci. Also sells accessories. Direct-from-the-manufacturer discounts available for the entire family.

Best Buys

A health and beauty-aid store carrying franchise cosmetics, fragrances, shampoo, and shave cream, along with sundry other items.

Bible Outlet

Carries all the Bibles from all the major publishers. Discounts from 10 to 50 percent off suggested retail prices. Also carries music cassettes, books, commentaries, dictionaries, study guides, children's books, and gifts.

Bike Athletic

The Bike brand communicates trust and reliability for quality sports products and apparel. Discounts of at least 30 percent.

Bikini World

Largest selection of ladies' and men's swimwear, including 125 styles at discount.

Black & Decker

Features quality reconditioned, blemished, and discontinued power tools; small appliances: personal-care products; and a full line of related accessories. Full factory warranty on power tools and appliances. Save 20 to 50 percent off suggested retail prices.

Bon Worth
Owned and operated by the manufacturer in Hendersonville, North Carolina, Bon Worth is a complete women's apparel store. Find the quality, price, and size you are looking for. Bon Worth carries petite, misses', and women's sizes up to size 46. Excellent selection of skirts, blouses, pants, jackets, sweaters, and activewear. Up to 60 percent savings every day.

Book Annex
Discounts on books, magazines, and cassette tapes. Carries books on tape, classical cassette tapes, current hard covers and paperbacks, children's books, publisher closeouts, and remainders. Magazines of all sorts.

Book Factory
A reader's delight at prices from pennies up.

Book Island
Books and paperbacks from 10 to 75 percent off retail prices, specializing in best-sellers, children's books, and books on the Civil War. Also carries magazines, tobacco, and sundries.

Bookland Book Outlet
More than 100,000 books to choose from, at discounts up to 90 percent. Huge savings on selected *New York Times* best-sellers. Savings on your favorite magazines and paperbacks. Every item in the store is discounted.

Book Sale
Huge savings on all titles.

Book Warehouse
The name says it all . . . 75,000 new books at 50 to 90 percent off publisher's retail prices. Vast selection of reading material for everyone includes children's books, cookbooks, and a complete business section. Best-sellers to topical reference in hardbound and paperback.

Boot Factory
Featuring Laredo and Code West boots as well as Australian Outback

dusters, Carolina work shoes, and western-influenced accessories. Factory-direct savings of up to 60 percent.

Boots, Etc
Up to 50 percent off on name brands.

Boots 'n Brims
Factory-direct prices on boots and western-style hats.

Boston Trader Kids
Value prices equal to the brand worn by Mom and Dad.

Boston Traders
Ladies' and men's clothing at 25 to 70 percent off regular retail prices.

Brass Exchange
Features a complete line of English antiques and fine brass giftware at affordable prices and savings of 30 to 60 percent.

Brass Factory
A variety of giftware at discount prices.

Brighter Side
Offers an extensive line of fine oil lamps, styled for both traditional and contemporary motifs, plus special models for outdoor use at up to 70 percent off retail prices. In addition, top-quality lamp oil is available in many colors and fragrances. Carries a complete line of accessory parts, including wicks, burners, and chimneys, as well as sconces and floral accent rings.

Brown Shoe Co.
Factory outlet offering selections of Naturalizer, Lifestride, Natural Sport, and Connie shoes at 30 to 50 percent savings.

Bruce Alan Bags
Better-quality leather goods, including hard- and soft-side luggage, backpacks, briefcases, attachés, handbags, wallets, umbrellas, and belts. Everyday prices are 25 to 75 percent off regular retail prices.

Bugle Boy
Women's, men's, and children's wear. Manufacturer's direct savings of 30 to 70 percent off retail.

Burlington Artists League Gallery
Burlington (North Carolina) works of art. Framed and matted paintings; other works of art to suit your budget.

Burlington Brands
Men's and women's casual apparel. Features first-quality and slightly imperfect apparel from thirty manufacturers, including such brands as Lands' End, Cross Creek, Haggar, Claude, Jantzen, Career Club, Lord Jeff, Robert Bruce, Pandora, Garland, Wrangler, and Munsingwear.

Burlington Coat Factory
Carries more than ten thousand coats year-round. Famous name brands and designer-label coats and apparel for the entire family at discount prices. Fine furs and leathers are included. Linens and shoes are sold as well.

Burlington Shoe
Men's and women's shoes; handbags. Discounted brand names include Aigner, Caressa, Westies, Capri, Reebok, Tretorn, Avia, Converse, Unisa, Jasmin, Nickels, Dexter, Nunn Bush, French Shriner, and Bass. Unusual sizes 4–4½ B.

Cabin Creek
Clothes, shoes, and Corningware.

Calvin Klein
Direct factory savings of 40 to 70 percent off retail prices every day. Casual sportswear for men and women. Designer collection for women.

Cannon Bed and Bath Outlet
An outlet of Fieldcrest/Cannon. Famous for factory-direct savings of 40 to 60 percent on irregular and discontinued styles.

Cannon Village Antique Mall
Antiques at 30 to 60 percent savings.

Cape Isle Knitters
Name-brand sweaters and knits, value priced. Finest quality, 100 percent cotton, contemporary knits for men and women, at 30 to 50 percent off retail prices.

Caper's. *See* $9.99 Stockroom.

Capezio
Shoes for women from the famous manufacturer at "direct" savings to you. Liz Claiborne, Evan Picone, Bandolino, Pappagallo, Capezio, and more.

Career Image
Professional womenswear at 25 to 70 percent off regular retail prices.

Carole Hochman Lingerie
Manufacturers of America's leading fashion intimate apparel. Savings on Christian Dior, Carole Hochman, and Sara Beth lingerie, plus Lily of France bras.

Carole Little
Designer women's career clothing, sportswear, and dresses at 40 to 75 percent off retail prices.

Carolina Clock & Rug
Clocks, oriental-design rugs, and other timeless items. Discounts by manufacturer, ranging from 25 to 70 percent off regular retail prices.

Carolina Interiors
Save 25 to 50 percent on more than three hundred of America's finest furniture lines. Interior-design service and worldwide shipping available.

Carolina Linens
Value-oriented fashions for bed and bath at 20 to 70 percent savings.

Carolina Pottery
"A Bargain EveryWare!" A warehouse selection of home decor and gift-

ware at discount prices. Flatware and dinnerware; wicker baskets and furniture; silk flowers and custom arranging; brass, crystal, and glassware; prints and custom framing; kitchen items; crafts; and much more, all at tremendous savings, at least 30 to 70 percent off regular retail prices.

Carousel Books
Twenty to seventy percent off unique and current books, including audio versions for the whole family. Wide variety of greeting cards, gifts, and goodies.

Carroll Reed
Catalog outlet offering modern classic women's clothing for all week long. Comfort and style at 20 to 50 percent off catalog prices.

Carter's
Factory-direct savings from the manufacturer of fine children's wear for more than a century. Offers a full line of children's playwear, sleepwear, and underwear, as well as layette products; sizes newborn to boys/girls 14. Savings from 30 to 60 percent always.

Casual Male Big & Tall
Save 25 to 70 percent off department-store prices on men's brand-name and designer fashions, especially in hard-to-fit sizes. Regular men's sizes and big and tall men's sizes are carried.

Century Curtain and Bedding Outlet
Discounts on fashions for your home.

Champion-Hanes
An outlet owned and operated by the manufacturer, offering a wide selection of Hanes Activewear for men and women and featuring first-quality products as well as imperfects. Always a wide variety of colorful sweats, T-shirts, and socks with direct-from-the-manufacturer pricing. Satisfaction is 100 percent guaranteed.

Chatham Country Store Outlet
Substantial savings on blankets, mattress pads, furniture upholstery,

throws, sheets, towels, bedspreads, place mats, pillows, and more. No refunds without receipt. Extra selections, with shipping, available.

Chaus
Updated fashion for petite, misses', and women's sizes at up to 70 percent off regular retail prices.

Childcraft
The authorized Disney outlet store. Toys and clothes at value prices.

Children's Outlet
Fashion clothing and accessories for children, sizes newborn to 14. Save 20 to 40 percent on famous brands, including OshKosh, Health-Tex, and Baby Togs.

Children's Place
Select from national brands and exclusive fashions for infants through teens. The company has a firm commitment to value and quality at a discount.

Christmas Factory
Huge savings on items to trim the tree and your house.

Churchill's
Brass pieces and a variety of small pieces of furniture (like nightstands) at savings of at least 10 percent. Discounts vary by manufacturer.

Cigarette-Magazine Outlet
Just as the name implies, at a 30 to 70 percent discount.

Clothesline
Junior apparel of name brands at 20 to 50 percent below department store prices.

Clothing Warehouse
A Da'nelle store—men's, women's, and children's clothing at manufacturer's wholesale prices. Jeans for the entire family.

Coach
From Coach Leatherware, handbags, belts, briefcases, business and personal accessories including wallets, organizers, and gloves, as well as silk ties and silk scarves for men and women.

Coats and Clark
Thread and sewing accessories at well below retail.

Cole-Haan
Fine men's, women's, and children's footwear and leather accessories. Savings at 35 percent or more.

Collector's Gallery
Mirrors, fine art, and prints at tremendous savings.

Colours
By Alexander Julian. Men's casual clothing. Savings of 30 to 60 percent every day.

Converse Shoe
Always 40 to 70 percent off complete lines of activewear and athletic footwear. Carries basketball, tennis, aerobics, training, walking, baseball, and football shoes and the world-famous "Chuck Taylor All Stars." Great savings on all children's shoes.

Corbin
Fine men's and women's clothing. A national trademark of quality and traditional style for more than forty years offering first-quality suits, trousers, skirts, jackets, and more.

Corning Factory Store, Corning Glass Works/Corning Revere
Excellent savings on Corningware, Pyrex, Corelle, Microwave Plus, Clear Advantage, Clear Elegance, and Crown Corning, from 20 to 50 percent off retail prices.

Country Road Australia
First-quality Australian-designed menswear, womenswear, and accessories. Savings of up to 75 percent off retail prices.

County Seat
A jeans store offering fashion denim and related jeanswear and casual apparel for juniors and young men for less.

Covers 'N Stuff
Quality bed and linen items at discount prices.

Crazy Horse
Substantial savings from an exclusive manufacturer's outlet of first-quality women's sportswear. Brands include Crazy Horse, Russ, and The Villager. Sizes include 4–16, misses', and petites.

Crown Jewels
A large inventory of fine fashion jewelry, featuring quality, selection, and value, with most items offered at 50 percent off the ticketed price.

CYA
Women's fashions and accessories at discount prices.

Damon/Enro
Prices reflect "direct from the factory to you." (Enro shirts are "Made in the USA," in Kentucky; the factory is in Louisville.) Merchandise emphasizes menswear, but some women's clothing is available. Carried are shirts, pants, sweaters, pajamas, coats, and accessories. Big and tall as well as regular sizes are included for men.

Dan River
Sheers, comforters, shams, dust ruffles, and window treatments in first-quality, closeouts, and slightly irregulars, all at substantial savings.

Dan's Factory Outlet
Large stock selection of current and surplus wallcovering. Approximately 25,000 to 30,000 rolls in stock with discounts on current patterns of 50 to 65 percent. Surplus wallcoverings from $3.49 to $9.99 per double roll. Brand names include Waverly, Seabrook, York, C&A, J. Chesterfield, Imperial, Mayfair, United, Burden, Coldroll, Village, Schumacher, Gramary, Carefree, Tattersall, Kinney, Sunwall, and Foremost. Large selection of oriental-style rugs at big savings. Large selection of

window shades. Specialize in "odd size" blinds that other stores do not stock. Benjamin Moore paint and shutters to complement discount decorating merchandise. All sales are final. Layaway plans available with one-third down. Extra selections may be ordered on merchandise.

Dansk

Savings to 60 percent on Dansk's classic tabletop designs: seconds, discontinued limited editions of dinnerware, teakwood, flatware, glassware, cookware, and gifts. Shipping through UPS available. March through Labor Day is Dansk's busiest time. End-of-summer markdowns and early Christmas buying are recommended. Mailing list maintained in store. Returns for exchange with receipt thirty days after purchase, or an in-store merchandise credit can be issued. Other merchandise may be acquired from other Dansk locales.

Danskin

Goods direct from the manufacturer at savings of 50 percent (and sometimes more) off everyday prices on women's and girls' activewear, including a complete assortment of leotards, tights, unitards, leg warmers, pantyhose, and lingerie. Ideal shopping for dance and activewear.

Designer Desk

Paper and school supplies at discounts of 30 to 60 percent off regular retail prices. Discounts vary by product.

designer's extras

Manufacturers for Joan Vass U.S.A. One hundred percent cotton-knit designs with the look and feel of cashmere, providing casual elegance for day-into-night or weekend dressing. Prices range from 40 to 60 percent off full retail amounts. The store also features a unique line of accessories to complement fashions.

Designer Silks, Etc.

Save up to 50 percent off this luxurious fashion statement.

Designer Sunglasses

"Looking" good for less. Off-price eyewear.

Dexter Shoes
A manufacturer's outlet that offers factory-direct savings on first-quality men's and women's shoes. Dexter is nationally recognized for leather dress and casual shoes that are proudly "Made in the USA." Save up to 50 percent on top-selling styles featured in retail stores nationwide.

Diamond Factory & Eelskin Outlet
A huge selection of beautiful designer rings—synthetic diamonds, cubic zirconias, genuine opals, onyx, and tigereye. Women's and men's styles with values to $99.50 offered at $19.95. See, too, the largest selection of turquoise and silver Indian jewelry in the East—and save up to 50 percent off retail prices. Genuine imported eelskin handbags, accessories, and shoes discounted up to 50 percent.

Diamond Jim's Jewelry
Huge savings on gold, silver, and jewels.

Diamonds Unlimited
Manufacturers of thousands of fine diamond, gemstone, and gold jewelry items. Save when you buy these items at the same wholesale prices that retail jewelers pay.

Dixie Belle Lingerie
Women's lingerie: bras, slips, panties, and some large sizes at direct-from-the-manufacturer discounts.

Dollartime
Jewelry, hair accessories, makeup, gift items, housewares, hardware, tapes and CDs, toys, and more, all at $1.00.

Dollar Tree
All items $1.00 or less every day. Value, variety, and quality on miscellaneous items.

Donnkenny
Related separates for career wear; sportswear, dresses, and sleepwear; all merchandise carried in both misses' and full-figure sizes. Prices are at least 50 percent off suggested retail amounts.

Dress Barn
Famous fashion labels, always at 25 to 70 percent off retail prices. Updated women's fashions of a wide variety, including casual and career wear, sweaters, pants, coats, suits, dresses, and accessories. Name brands include Liz Claiborne, Silk and Company, Guess, Claude, Cherokee, Christopher, Sasson, Kasper, Atrium, Rumors, Nilani, Melrose, Michael Blair, Betsy's Things, Seque, Jones/New York, Jennifer Reed, Panther, Dawn Joy, Scarlett, Mark Richards, Erica, Lee David, and Rafaella. Sizes 3/4 to 15/16 with some petite. (The Burlington, North Carolina, location is the "consolidation store," meaning that at the beginning of each season, all Dress Barn store merchandise nationwide is sent there to move out.)

Dress Barn Woman
Full-cut womenswear at 25 to 70 percent off regular retail prices.

Dress Ups!
Fashion jewelry, watches, scarves, and accessories for all occasions at a 30 to 40 percent discount.

Duck Head
The emblem that has become famous for men's, women's, children's, and toddler's casual wear, plus handbags, toys, and jewelry. First- and second-quality merchandise from 20 to 50 percent off retail. Discounts vary. Exchanges with cash register receipt only.

Ducks Unlimited
Menswear at 25 to 70 percent off regular retail prices.

Eagle's Eye
Women's and children's classic sportswear; women's sleepwear for less. All first quality and all in season.

Eagle's Eye Kids
Fine-quality, classic children's apparel. Innovative store designed to entertain children while adults shop at value prices.

Easy Spirit & Co.
The right shoes for all walking women. Factory-direct savings of 50 per-

cent every day on the first dress pump with a walking shoe built right inside and on the Easy Spirit Walking Shoe, crafted with twenty unique features for exceptional support.

Eddie Bauer
Save 30 to 70 percent every day on merchandise from America's premier outdoor outfitter.

Electronic Express
Featuring a full line of audio and video equipment, telephones, answering machines, and accessories at up to 50 percent off suggested retail.

Electronics Outlet
Name-brand electronic products for car, home, office, and on-the-go. Home and car stereo equipment, telephones, radar detectors, CBs, and accessories. All fully warranted and discounted up to 75 percent.

Ellen Tracy
Features better women's apparel, concentrating on giving successful working women clothes that are well made and fashionable without being trendy.

Etienne Aigner
Designer looks in leather at discounts of at least 30 percent off suggested retail prices.

Euro Collections/Bleyle
Superior quality womenswear direct from their own factories in America and Europe at 35 to 70 percent off regular retail prices.

Evan-Picone
Owned and operated by Palm Beach Company, offering first-quality, name-brand apparel at savings of 35 to 70 percent off regular retail prices. Current-season styles in tailored clothing, sportswear, and accessories for men and women. Labels include Evan-Picone, Palm Beach, Gant, Eagle, Austin Hill, and Haspel.

Everything but Water
An entirely new approach to swimwear. Choose from more than five

thousand swimsuits, coordinating cover-ups, and related accessories. Also has an "outrageous" gift department. All set in a unique atmosphere, complete with sales staff modeling swimwear.

Everything's A Dollar
. . . and they mean it! General, variety-store merchandise with a surprise around every corner—"5 & 10's" were never this much fun!

Eyewear House
Glasses at 25 to 70 percent off regular retail prices.

Factory Connection
Women's fashions and sportswear at great prices.

Factory Linens
A real factory-owned and -operated linen store. Quality selection of kitchen, table, bed, and bath linens, and related accessories, all discounted.

Fall's Custom-Jewelry
At least 30 to 60 percent off regular prices (varies by selection).

Famous Brands Housewares
From kitchen to closet, gadgets to storage, entertaining to decorating—name-brand items to outfit your home at outlet prices.

Famous Footwear
More than twenty thousand pairs of shoes for the entire family, at everyday savings of 10 to 70 percent. First-quality athletic and dress shoes whose lines include Mushroom, Candies, Reebok, Nike, Nunn Bush, Connie, Sporto, L.A. Gear, Jazzman, and Jacqueline.

Famous Name Brand Shoes
Offers fashion and trendy styles, athletic and work shoes, by major manufacturers. Discounted styles include Aigner, Bass, 9 West, SAS, Soft Spots, Lifestride, Naturalizer, Nike, Reebok, Adidas, Rockport, Bostonian, Freeman, and E. T. Wright. Best times to shop: June, August, and December. Sizes: ladies', 4–13; children's, 10–5; men's, 6–15. Layaways at no extra charge. Extra selections may be ordered.

Fancy Free Kids
Children's clothing at 25 to 70 percent off regular retail prices.

Farah
Home of the well-known slacks manufacturer . . . at discount prices.

Farberware, Inc.
Savings from 25 to 60 percent on America's quality brand-name stainless steel cookware and electric kitchen appliances. Will ship anywhere in the United States.

Fashion Direct
Save 30 to 70 percent on women's office apparel, sportswear, and sweaters. Petite, misses', and plus sizes, too.

Fashion Flair
Savings starting at 40 to 60 percent off manufacturers' suggested retail prices on men's, women's, and children's apparel. Famous brands like Izod, Lacoste, and Monet direct from the factory.

Fashion Mart
Handcrafted clothing for today's fashion-minded woman for less. The crocheted tops, skirts, and one- and two-piece dresses are elegant and will fit into anyone's wardrobe. Also offers embroidered skirts, tops, and dresses and unique cutwork dresses and tops.

Fieldcrest/Cannon
Top-styled home textile products with savings of 40 to 60 percent or more on Fieldcrest/Cannon towels, sheets, pillowcases, bedspreads, comforters, blankets, bath rugs and sets, and kitchen accessories. Excellent prices as well on bed pillows, mattress pads, shower curtains, and accessories for the bathroom and bedroom. Selection includes imperfects and first-quality closeouts.

Fila
Sport and fitness footwear, apparel, and accessories at a discount.

Finish Line
Outstanding prices and selection on athletic shoes and clothing, including Adidas, Converse, Foot-Joy, Ocean Pacific, Puma, and Fila.

First Choice
A great selection of European sportswear at savings of up to 65 percent off retail prices. Featured are Escada, Laurel, and Crisca by designer Margaretha Ley.

Fitz and Floyd
Features world-renowned Fitz and Floyd dinnerware, giftware, and decorative accessories for the home at real factory outlet prices; also giftware by Omnibus Collection International, fine crystal, and brass.

Florsheim Shoe
The very best in men's shoes at savings from 20 to 50 percent off retail prices.

Foot Factory
Shoes at 25 to 70 percent off regular retail prices.

Footprints
Savings of at least 30 to 60 percent on fine footwear.

Forever Yours
Cards and gifts at discount prices.

Formfit
Direct from the factory. Save 30 to 70 percent off retail prices on better-quality merchandise every day. Studio 36 dresses; Appel long and short robes, leisure wear, and sweat suits; Smart Time women's dusters; Myonne panties; and Formfit bras, slips, panties, camisoles, and girdles.

Fostoria
Substantial savings on all discontinued and selected irregular glassware. Company clearances feature lead crystal stemware, giftware, tableware, dinnerware, and colored casual stemware.

Fragrance Cove
Discounts on perfumes from designers and other well-known brands. Cosmetics, too, at 15 to 60 percent off.

Frugal Frank's Shoe Outlet
Features famous name-brand athletic, dress, and casual footwear for the entire family. Expect 20 to 40 percent off regular retail prices.

Fruit of the Loom
Ladies' and men's clothing at 25 to 70 percent off regular retail prices.

Fuller Brush
Bargains on items produced by the most famous name in brush manufacturing.

Full Size Fashions
Clothing for the full-size woman, including styles by Smith & Jones, Koret, Pykett, Lady Devon, Fire Islander, Chaus Woman, and Levi Bendovers. Assorted sweaters, blouses, and jeans. Save from 30 to 60 percent off regular prices. Featured are sizes 16½–32½ and 30–52.

Gals Direct
First-quality junior fashions in the latest styles, discounted.

Galt Sand
Manufacturer of upscale activewear featuring sweatshirts, pants, hoods, T-shirts, and shorts at a savings of 30 to 70 percent off suggested retail prices.

General Bookstore
Values in all types of reading material.

General Shoe Factory to You
Factory owned and operated, selling direct to the consumer from the factory at 20 to 50 percent below the regular retail price. Expect Genesco's famous brands, as well as many other labels.

Generra Sportswear
All current season's fashions for young men and women and boys and girls at 25 to 70 percent savings off suggested retail prices.

Genesco Factory to You Store
An outlet for one of the nation's leading manufacturers and retailers in the shoe industry. Nationally advertised men's and women's shoes at savings of 35 to 50 percent off regular retail prices.

Geoffrey Beene
Fashions from a popular American designer. Select from dressy, casual, and relaxed life-styles . . . 20 to 70 percent off retail prices.

Georgia Wholesale Furniture
Furnish your house for less.

Gift Corner
Offers a fine selection of gifts—Williamsburg sterling, Delft, china, crystal, and brass at below retail.

Gift Depot
Twenty-five to 70 percent off regular retail prices on gifts to give and for the home.

Gilligan & O'Malley
Women's quality sleepwear, robes, and loungewear at savings of 40 to 60 percent or more. Purchase directly from the manufacturer at a fraction of the full retail price.

Gitano
First-quality, direct-from-the-manufacturer savings and up to 50 percent off department-store prices on Gitano's famous lines of casual sportswear and activewear in junior sizes 3–13, misses' sizes 8–18, and plus sizes 32–42; men's sizes 28–42; and, in the Eva Joia line, girls' sizes 4–6X and 7–14. Features the latest fashions in tops, pants, skirts, dresses, jeans, swimwear, outerwear, shoes, underwear, handbags, and accessories.

Gitano/Kids
Famous Gitano fashions for kids, all at tremendous savings. First-quality merchandise direct from the manufacturer, featuring the latest fashions for children.

Gold and Diamonds Direct
A source for buying the highest-quality fine jewelry direct from the manufacturer and importer. Offers the latest styles, a large selection, and factory-direct prices. Full-service jewelry repair on premises; custom designs; professional appraisals.

Gold & Gem Outlet
Fine jewelry, factory-direct: "Never pay retail again." Save from 50 to 70 percent. Italian gold chains. Jewelry repair.

Gold & Silver Connection
Fine jewelry at 25 to 70 percent off regular retail prices.

Gold Market
Diamonds, gold, watches at 50 percent off retail prices.

Gold Outlet
Twenty-five to 70 percent off regular retail prices on gold jewelry.

Gold Rush
Fourteen-carat gold and sterling silver chains, charms, and earrings at 20 to 40 percent off retail prices, with a one-year guarantee. Other inventory includes fashionable costume jewelry.

Goldsmith Shop
Fine jewelry, diamonds, semiprecious stones, plus watches at significant discounts.

Gold Toe
Dress, casual, and athletic socks for men, women, and boys. Great savings on this name brand.

Golf Outlet
Needs for "the game" at a discount.

Goodwin Weavers
Home furnishings at 20 to 50 percent off regular retail prices. Featuring the Bob Timberlake collection including framed art, furniture, cotton afghans, linens, and accessories.

Gorham
Savings on seconds, overstocks, discontinued patterns, and limited editions of the manufacturer's fine china dinnerware, crystal stemware, sterling and stainless steel flatware, silver hollowware, porcelain figurines and dolls, and crystal and silver gifts.

Great Western Boot
Boots and authentic western wear at a discount.

Greetings 'N' More
Save 50 to 75 percent off retail prices on all your greeting-card, paper, and party needs. Nationally known brands include products such as cards, gift wrap, stationery, candles, party supplies, seasonal decorations, and more.

Guess?
What else? Jeanswear and other Guess? wear at between 30 and 70 percent off suggested retail prices. Products for men, women, and children.

Guven Fine Jewelry
Substantial savings on gold and silver.

Habersham Vintners & Winery
Wine tasting and sales; Georgia premium wines.

Hamilton Luggage and Handbags
Luggage and handbags for less. Name-brand luggage includes Hartmann, Samsonite, Skyway, Ventura, Lark, Amelia, and Earhart; name-brand handbags include Aigner and Stone Mountain. Also carried are name-brand wallets (Buxton, Prince Gardner, and Bosca) and Aigner shoes (sizes 5½–6 only). Expect a savings of 30 to 60 percent off retail prices.

Hamrick's
Name-brand fashions for women, men, and children at extra-low factory outlet and discount prices. Famous for manufactured labels: Nikki, Southern Lady, LINKS and Company collection.

Handbag Company
Huge selection of quality handbags discounted.

Hanes Mill
Discounted women's hosiery, socks, lingerie, and activewear; men's underwear and socks. Name brands include Bali bras and L'eggs hosiery.

harvé benard
A wide selection of designer women's apparel and accessories at dramatic savings. Also features a full line of men's furnishings. Stylish savings on business and casual wardrobes; seasonal favorites available in every size. Pay 30 to 60 percent less than suggested retail prices.

Hathaway Shirt
Merchandise for men includes Hathaway dress and sport shirts, Christian Dior sportswear and elegant dress shirts, and Chaps and Ralph Lauren sportswear. Wide selection of men's ties and women's White Stag sportswear. Olga and Warner's are the lines of intimate apparel for women. Prices are 40 percent or more off manufacturer's suggested retail amounts.

Hats Etc.
"Top" off that favorite outfit and add just the right accessories at 30 to 60 percent off regular retail prices.

Helen's Handbags
America's handbags and accessories bargains.

Henson Lingerie
An outlet offering Henson lingerie, exclusively, with factory-direct pricing.

Heritage Fine Jewelry
A sparkling array of fine gold and silver jewelry. On-site custom design.

HE-RO Group

Manufacturer of women's designer apparel featuring Oleg Cassini, Bob Mackie, and Bill Blass. Collections include evening wear, leather and suede dresses, and sportswear, all at a savings of 30 to 70 percent off department-store prices.

Hickory Oriental Rug Gallery

Consumers can save up to 60 percent on better-quality handmade oriental rugs imported from India, China, Romania, Pakistan, and Iran; additional savings on discontinued patterns and samples. Wool piles, Dhurries, kilims, rounds, squares, and runners are some of the stock varieties. Sizes range from 2-by-3 to 10-by-14 feet; other sizes are stocked in the warehouse. Special sizes can be ordered. A "shop by mail" service allows customers to mail their floor plans and color samples and receive the appropriate oriental rug by return shipment. Custom shapes and sizes are available; shipment is nationwide. Return policy: if item is defective, with receipt within six months. Extra selections of merchandise may be ordered if not in stock.

Hilton Head Shirt

The island's largest discount source for unique imprinted sportswear, hats, souvenirs, and gifts, along with the most exclusive T-shirts and sweatshirts.

Hit or Miss

"Where Fashion Costs Less." Offers current-season, first-quality, brand-name career and casual fashions at prices 20 to 50 percent below the regular prices of leading stores in the area. Coats, sweaters, and accessories are also available.

Home Fashions Outlet

Factory-direct closeouts and slightly irregulars at 60 to 70 percent off manufacturer's suggested retail prices on bedspreads, comforters, curtains, pillows, kitchen accessories, piece goods, and more. Returns for merchandise credit only.

HomeMaker Bedspread Outlet

Factory store for Carolina Creations, Carrington, and Sheridan, plus the

HomeMaker label. Bedspreads, comforters, sheets, window treatments for the home, at 50 to 60 percent off department-store prices. Return policy: Return within five days of purchase for exchange. Allow five days for refunds over $50. Free layaway! Extra selections can be ordered.

Hush Puppies
The "quiet" shoe at prices to whisper about—25 to 70 percent off regular retail prices.

I. B. Diffusion
Womenswear for work, play, and elegant evenings. Plus sizes, too. Discounted brands include I. B. Diffusion and Joye & Fun.

Import-Export Exchange
Elegant eelskin goods. Eelskin is said to be 150 percent stronger and softer than other leathers. Save 35 to 70 percent on first-line eelskin goods and accessories.

Interior Alternative
Fabric, wallpaper, comforter sets, bedspreads, dust ruffles, pillow shams, and decorative pillows. Save 30 to 70 percent on famous brands including Schumacher, Waverly, Gramercy, Village, and Fieldcrest. Restocking constantly, with highest stock levels from February through November. Mailing list kept. All sales final.

International Silver
Stunning place settings, cutlery, and gifts from Towle, International Silver, and Wallace Silversmiths. Discounts vary by brand.

Islandgear
Save up to 60 percent on Islandwear and many other nationally recognized brands of swimwear for men and women. More than twenty-five hundred first-quality suits every day. Women's Islandgear also features beach towels and related items. The collection of activewear and casual wear found at Islandgear is one of the best values for completing your vacation wardrobe. Men's and women's sizes 6–45.

Island Shirt
Quality 100 percent cotton Hilton Head printed T-shirts for men, women, and children. Souvenirs, hats, and sunglasses at a discount.

Island Wear/Swimsuit Source
Everyday savings of up to 60 percent on Islandwear and many other nationally recognized brands of swimwear for men, women, and children. Also offers casual wear. First-quality styles include boy legs, bra cups, skirts, and bikinis. Sizes 6–46.

Izod
Save from 30 to 50 percent off manufacturer's suggested retail prices on men's and boys' sportswear. Lacoste also is carried.

Jaymar
Excellent values on Jaymar and Sansabelt and a complete line of men's apparel. Some big and tall sizes available at 25 to 70 percent off regular retail prices.

JC Penney Catalog Outlet
First-quality merchandise from the Penney distribution network at everyday discount prices. This is a "real outlet store with real outlet pricing." Family apparel, home furnishings, and many specialty items at discount prices. Merchandise constantly replenished to offer customers the very best values. "We stand behind what we sell. We are never satisfied until the customer is satisfied."

J. Crew
Classic designer clothing for men and women at savings of 30 to 50 percent from one of the best-loved catalog retailers.

Jerzees
Discounts vary on T-shirts, sweatshirts, fleecewear, activewear, leisure wear, and resort wear direct from the factory. Also offers an exciting collection of transfer prints to be applied to the garment of your choice.

Jewel Mart USA
Jewelry manufacturer's outlet offering Sieko, Citizen, Speidel, Black Hills Gold, Ray-Ban, and gold by gram weight. Layaways available.

Jewelry Kingdom
Contemporary fashion accessories at 25 to 70 percent off regular retail prices.

Jewelry Outlet
America's most popular contemporary fashion jewelry lines, famous name-brand watches, clocks, fourteen-karat gold jewelry, sterling silver, jewel boxes, sunglasses, and belts. Discounts vary by manufacturer.

J. G. Hook
Features a full line of women's and petite better classic sportswear, coats, blazers, shirts, sweaters, and more, priced at least 33 to 50 percent off retail amounts.

J. H. Collectibles
Sells coordinating sportswear and separates in sizes 2–16, plus a great line of petites, all from 30 to 60 percent off suggested retail price. Customers can mix and match garments according to fabrics and colors.

Joan & David
Handcrafted leather footwear and accessories of the finest quality, with intriguing proportions and unusual combinations of color and material.

Jockey
Underwear, hosiery, sleepwear, robes, sportswear, and sweaters—values for the entire family.

Jody's Accessories
Costume jewelry at 25 to 70 percent off regular retail prices.

Johnston & Murphy
"Top of the line" in men's footwear . . . at "bottom of the barrel" discounts. Enjoy a fine selection of men's dress, casual, and golf shoes, plus a unique collection of accessories.

Jonathan Logan
First-quality, current-season women's sportswear, dresses, activewear, swimwear, and more; expect from 25 to 70 percent off retail prices.

Name brands include Villager, Aigner, Chaus, Personal, Action Scene, Fritzi of California, Leslie Fay, Breckenridge, Bill Blass Swimwear, Cali, and Positive Attitude. (Other brands may be included and vary from store to store.) Petite, misses', and women's sizes.

Jones New York
Womenswear at 25 to 70 percent off regular retail prices.

Jordache
The name in jeans . . . at discounts.

Judy Bond Blouses
A true manufacturer's outlet, with savings of up to 75 percent off suggested retail prices. Blouses in petite sizes 4–14, misses' sizes 6 18, and Ms. Bond sizes 36–46. A special selection of sportswear at everyday discount prices.

Just Kids
A complete line of Her Majesty girls' sportswear, sleepwear, swimwear, slips, and panties, plus name-brand clothing for boys (infant through 16) and girls (infant through 14). Also offers children's accessories, tennis and jogging shoes, and hosiery for the entire family. Savings of up to 50 percent or more.

K & S Men's Liquidation
Men's clothing at closeout prices.

Keith's Record Shop
Discounts on records, tapes, stereo equipment, bumper stickers, and greeting cards. Will special-order.

Kelly's Kids
Up to 50 percent off on children's wear.

Kelly Stryker
Specializing in ladies' sportswear and dresses that exhibit high quality at affordable prices. Sportswear in denim, printed denim, and cotton and rayon reflect an informal life-style that women of all ages can wear. Products crafted in the USA.

Kids Biz

Quality name-brand children's outerwear, ranging from newborn to girls' size 14 and boys' size 18. Play area for kids. Save 20 to 40 percent off suggested retail prices.

Kid's Collection

Up to 50 percent off on children's wear.

King Clock Company

Makers of solid-wood grandfather clocks, wall clocks, mantel clocks, and cuckoo clocks, with some German movements.

King Frog

Discount prices on clothing, shoes, and accessories. First-quality, current fashions. Largest selection of all-weather coats in the area.

Kitchen Collection

Kitchenware, cookware, gadgets, and accessories for the gourmet in you. The exclusive factory outlet for Wear-Ever cookware and Proctor-Silex appliances. Offers the widest selection of first-quality products, as well as selected manufacturer seconds and closeout items, all at factory-direct savings. Save 20 to 70 percent off comparable retail prices.

Kitchen Place

A full line of household items, textiles, and gifts: Ecko, Rubbermaid, Pfaltzgraff china, International china, Wear-Ever, Corning, Pyrex, Litton, Toscany, Mikasa crystal, WP&G crystal, and Longchamp crystal.

Knife Factory

Cover your kitchen utility needs and find recreational pieces, at prices that are a "cut" below retail.

Knits by K.T.

A factory-owned and -operated store, featuring current-season, first-quality women's sweaters and knit tops by Kenneth Too and sportswear by other famous makers. Expect 25 to 60 percent off regular retail prices every day. Misses' and large sizes.

K-Town Furniture
Brand-name furniture and appliances at low outlet prices. Ship worldwide.

Kuppenheimer Men's Clothiers
A manufacturer of finely tailored men's suits, sport coats, and slacks in the United States, offering excellent-value prices.

Land & Sea Leather
Exotic leathers at 25 to 50 percent off regular retail prices.

L & S Shoes
Carries a wide variety of fashions in name-brand shoes for men and women. The latest styles, and all at prices 20 to 60 percent off suggested retail.

Langtry
Discounted womenswear.

Laura Ashley
This famous name brand is offered at 25 to 70 percent off regular retail prices.

Leather by S. Mullins
Manufacturer and distributor of fine leather goods since 1969. Handbags, belts, wallets, and footwear.

Leather Loft
Luxury leather for less. Choose from a varied selection of luggage, briefcases, handbags, wallets, belts, executive gifts, and designer accessories at 40 to 60 percent off regular retail prices.

Le Creuset
The famous cast-iron cookware from France, at 60 percent savings.

L'eggs/Hanes/Bali
An exclusive outlet for these famous name-brand lines that may include

merchandise with slight imperfections, closeouts, and overstocks. Save 20 to 50 percent (or more) on first-quality hosiery, lingerie, socks, underwear, and miscellaneous items.

Lenox
Enjoy extraordinary savings on elegant selected seconds of Lenox china and crystal. Distinctive handcrafted gifts, Hartmann luggage, candles, silver plate, and other tabletop accessories. Mailing list is maintained within each store. Return policy: thirty days with receipt.

Leslie Fay
Direct manufacturer of famous-label dresses, suits, sportswear, designer-wear, and activewear in misses', petites, and large sizes at prices 25 to 70 percent off regular retail.

Levi's
The jean at value prices. A complete "Levis Only" department store for the entire family, with the widest selection of sizes and styles at 50 percent off retail prices. Levi jeans, Dockers, shirts, blouses, and jackets.

Libbey Glass Factory Outlet
Glasses, tumblers, pitchers, bowls, and more. Factory-direct value prices.

Linens 'n Things
A specialty linen store featuring quality brand-name merchandise from leading designers and manufacturers. Prices at 20 to 40 percent off regular retail amounts. "We beat white sales every day." Towels, sheets, comforters, bathroom accessories, and much more. Everything for the bedroom and bath.

Lingerie Shoppe
Save up to 50 percent off retail prices on lingerie.

Little Red Shoe House (Wolverine)
Choose from a wide selection of fashionable, name-brand footwear for the entire family at savings of 20 to 50 percent off suggested retail

prices. Owned and operated by Wolverine World Wide of Rockford, Michigan. Lines for adults include Hush Puppies, Wolverine work boots, Brooks athletic shoes, and Coleman Outdoor; lines for children include Pony, Converse, Adidas, Reebok, and L.A. Gear athletic shoes.

Liz Claiborne
Substantial savings on wear-now selections. Discounted first-quality merchandise, including dresses and sportswear for misses and petite sizes, handbags and fashion accessories, and Claiborne menswear, sportswear, and furnishings.

L.J.'s Fashions
Contemporary fashions for women. Famous labels at factory prices.

London Fog
Carry only London Fog products, which include rainwear and coats, children's coats, wool and leather jackets, sweaters, shirts, luggage, umbrellas, hats, and scarves. A 50 percent discount (or more) on inventory.

Love's Diamond and Jewelry
Fine jewelry and gift items at discount prices.

Lumberton Outlet Flea Market
A variety bazaar of items at 30 to 70 percent off regular retail prices.

Magnavox
Save 25 to 70 percent off retail prices every day on color televisions, projection televisions, computers, portable audio, VCRs, and stereo components.

Maidenform
Intimate apparel: bras, lingerie, panties, and sleepwear. Save up to 60 percent.

Manhattan
More than just a shirt store. Offers savings of up to 70 percent off suggested retail prices every day on first-quality, brand-name sportswear for men and women. Men's brands include Manhattan, John Henry, and

Perry Ellis; women's brands include Manhattan and Lady Arrow. Some plus and petite sizes.

M.C. Sox
Family sock connection . . . factory-direct socks at factory-direct prices.

Menswear, Inc.
Better men's clothing, sportswear, furnishings, and activewear. Only the finest, most fashionable merchandise is chosen for this store, which offers fantastic savings.

Merchandise Warehouse
Gifts and accessories for the home and office at 20 to 70 percent off suggested retail prices. Jewelry, crystal, lamps, clocks, and more.

Micki Designer Separates
Designer women's suit separates in sizes 2–18, plus washable silk dresses and blouses at 20 to 50 percent off retail prices.

Mikasa
A factory outlet that features a tremendous selection of dinnerware, stemware, flatware, table linen, and giftware direct from the manufacturer, as well as merchandise from other internationally famous designers. Save up to 80 percent.

Multiples
Ladies' knitwear in mix-and-match colors. Expect at least 30 percent discounts.

Music 4 Less
. . . but not less quality. Discounts vary by artist and label.

Napier
This brand-name jewelry is offered at 40 percent off full retail prices.

Naturalizer, Etc.
Famous name-brand shoes at 25 to 70 percent off regular retail prices.

Nautica
Fashion apparel that reflects the casual attitude of life outdoors. First-quality current styles for men and women at 30 to 50 percent off original prices.

Nautical Nook
Seaworthy savings at 25 to 70 percent off regular retail prices.

NCS Shoe
Save 25 to 70 percent on top-of-the-line women's footwear.

Necklace Factory
Uniquely designed necklaces made on the premises, offered at prices substantially below retail, plus a large selection of earrings. Browsers welcome.

Nettle Creek
Your source for an assortment of custom-decorating products. Offers a variety of bedspreads, decorator pillows, fabric by the yard, and custom-made window dressings. In addition, accessories such as dust ruffles, pillow shams, upholstered headboards, and boudoir furniture are available or can be custom-made at the customer's request. Up to 35 percent off retail prices.

Newport
"The Factory Store for Men." Save 35 percent or more every day on current-season, first-quality coordinated sportswear, shirts, sweaters, activewear, and outerwear. Owned and operated by one of America's largest sportswear manufacturers.

Nickels
Women's quality fashion footwear at 30 to 70 percent off department-store prices. Featuring Nickels, Via Spiga, Paloma, Jazz, Studio Paolo, and Glacee Brands.

Nike/Sports Outlet/Reebok
Prices are approximately 40 to 60 percent off retail prices. Carries "Nike Air" for both men and women and other shoes designed for running,

basketball, and tennis. Sportswear for men and women includes shirts, shorts, sweatpants, warm-ups, running tights, tanks, and socks. Children's wear and shoes, beginning at size 2 infant, are offered. Gym bags are also available.

Nilani
The store features misses' sizes 2–14, women's sizes 16–24, and petite sizes. Dresses suitable for almost any occasion, silks, coordinated separates, and sportswear by Billy Jack. Prices range from 20 to 60 percent off suggested retail.

Nina's Accessory World
Accessories at 25 to 70 percent off regular retail prices.

$9.99 Stockroom
Just what the name implies. Off-price, value-oriented women's clothing.

9 West
Ladies' footwear for every occasion at savings of 30 percent or more.

No Nonsense & More
Save from 30 to 70 percent on pantyhose, socks, and lingerie.

Nutrition Outlet
Everything for the health- and fitness-conscious shopper—vitamins, supplements, natural foods and cosmetics, proteins, and a full line of fitness and weight equipment. Everything discounted.

Oak Towne Furniture
Discounts on fine-crafted oak furniture.

Ocean Galleries
Pictures, lamps, baskets, wicker furniture, silk arrangements, table accessories, and sports prints. Discounts by manufacturer of at least 20 percent.

Old Mill
The exclusive factory outlet for one of America's leading manufacturers

of women's apparel. Labels include Country Suburban and Weather-vane. Offers updated coordinates and contemporary separates in sizes 4–18 (petite sizes 4–16). Savings range from 25 to 70 percent.

Old Time Pottery
" . . . just like Grandma used to have!" Old-time quality, too, at today's modern discounts. Discounts vary, but expect at least 20 percent off retail prices.

Olga/Warner's
Everyday savings of 30 percent and more on famous-maker/designer and better intimate apparel. Assortment includes first-quality bras, panties, slips, and sleepwear from Olga, Warner's, Ungars, Blanche, and Scassi.

One $ Store
That's right! Everything in this variety store is only $1.00.

Oneida
Huge savings on stainless and silver-plated flatware, hollowware, baby items, and gifts direct to you from Oneida Silversmiths, at 25 to 70 percent off regular retail prices.

Oneita
Clothes for the entire family at 25 to 70 percent off regular retail prices.

One Price Clothing
Ladies' wear . . . all at 25 to 70 percent off regular retail prices.

Optical Outlet
Prescription eyewear and accessories. More than eight hundred frames to choose from, including fashion and designer frames. Top-quality lenses. Single vision $49, bifocals $64, trifocals $79; Ray-Ban sunglasses $33–$48. Eyes examined.

Orbit
Misses' and women's sportswear from Season Ticket at discount prices.

OshKosh B'Gosh (The Genuine Article)
Everyday savings of 20 to 50 percent off retail prices on a complete line of children's sportswear, swimwear, and shoes for boys and girls. Also workwear and menswear. "Made in the USA."

Outerbanks
Sportswear and more at a discount.

Outlet Marketplace
Thirty to 70 percent off Lee jeans; sweats; activewear for the entire family; Health-Tex children's wear; sleepwear; and underwear.

Outlet Unlimited
Varied discounts on bedspreads, curtains, crafts of all types, silk flowers, brass, ribbon, lace, pictures, baskets, paints, and jewelry crafts. New merchandise comes in daily. Two-day return policy. No cash refunds: exchange or credit slips. Thirty-day layaway plans. Extra selections of merchandise may be ordered.

Owl-o-Rest
Furniture, lamps, pictures, and accessories. Save 20 to 40 percent on furniture brands including Bassett, Lexington, Rowe, and Stanley. Lamps, pictures, and accessories may be returned with receipt. Layaways available for ninety days, no interest. Extra selections of merchandise may be ordered.

Palm Beach
Savings from 30 to 50 percent and more off manufacturer's suggested retail prices on men's Palm Beach suits and sport coats, men's dress and casual pants, Gant dress and sport shirts, sweaters, ties, and outerwear. Ladies' Evan-Picone collections including blazers, skirts, slacks, blouses, and sweaters; ladies' Monet, Trifari, and Marvella jewelry. Boys' Izod and Gant sportswear.

Palmetto Textile/Linen Outlet
First-quality towels, sheets, rugs, and more from Cannon, Fieldcrest, Martex, and Springs, as well as select imports from China and India, at 25 to 60 percent off regular retail prices.

Paper Factory

A paper store for all occasions: party goods and decorations, gift wrap and accessories, paper supplies for home and office, and books, games, and puzzles. Savings of up to 50 percent.

Patchington

Unique resort and travel fashion. Sizes 2–16. Twenty to 90 percent off retail prices.

Paul Revere Shoppe

Revereware teakettles and cookware; gadgets, copper, and assorted gift items for less.

Perfumania

Designer names and other popular scents. Discounts vary according to availability and manufacturer.

Perry Ellis

The celebrated lines of Perry Ellis fashion for men and women. Lines are first quality, in-season, and include Signature, Collection, Portfolio, and America.

Petite Shop

If you are five-foot-four or under and wear sizes 2–14, the fashions are proportioned to fit you perfectly without alterations. Everything is discounted 20 to 50 percent or more off manufacturers' retail prices.

Pfaltzgraff

Features twelve stoneware patterns, as well as coordinating home fragrances, lamps, and glassware. Discounts vary but usually are 20 to 50 percent off retail prices. Also features a vast array of gift and special collection pieces. All stoneware products are safe for freezer, oven, and dishwasher use.

Phidippides

Men's sportswear at discounts. Discounts vary by manufacturer; expect 30 to 60 percent off regular retail prices.

Picture Framer
Discounts on framing for your favorite art or photographs.

Piece Goods
Value-oriented fabrics and notions.

Pixie Playmates
Children's clothing, sizes infant to 14, at 40 to 70 percent off regular retail. Special $1.00 sales in the fall. Mailing list maintained. Exchanges for credit only.

Player's World of Golf
Professional golf equipment, clothing, and accessories, plus other sports clothing and equipment at the guaranteed lowest prices anywhere. Tennis and beach clothing, leisure wear, and dancewear, featuring Fila, Head, Quantum, and other lines.

Plumm's (E.J.)
Designer and famous-maker fashions for the contemporary woman. Discounted 20 to 50 percent off manufacturer's retail prices every day. Sizes 3–15 and 4–16.

Polly Flinders
Hand-smocked girls' dresses, sizes newborn to 14, known across the country for their beauty and quality. Savings of 40 to 60 percent on girls' and infants' shoes, dresses, panties, tights, and sleepwear.

Polo/Ralph Lauren
In addition to traditional wear for men and women and roughwear for the entire family, the outlet also carries the complete Polo/Ralph Lauren line of home furnishings, fragrances, shoes, and accessories, all discounted 25 to 50 percent off suggested retail prices.

President's Tailor
Custom-made suits from a selection of English fabrics and linings. Expert alterations and restyling of clothes for men and women at value prices.

Prestige Fragrance & Cosmetics, PFC Fragrance
Prestigious brands of men's and women's fragrances, toiletries, and cosmetics, priced at 25 to 60 percent off the suggested retail value.

Price Jewelers
Owned and operated by a jewelry manufacturer. Offers a large selection of fine jewelry at 20 to 50 percent off retail prices on such famous names as Seiko, Citizen, Colibri, and Cross. Lines include fine diamonds, gold, and fourteen-carat fashion jewelry.

Princess Handbags
Handbags, belts, luggage, and wallets. Discounted brand names include Adolpho, Samsonite, Ballanciaga, Sasson, Sunco eelskin, Stone Mountain, Phillippe, Borelli, Brute, Jordache, and Buxton.

Publisher's Book Outlet/Card Barn
Current paperbacks, hard covers, and *New York Times* best-sellers at 10 to 25 percent savings. Cards, gift wrap, party items, and invitations are always at a 10 percent savings.

Publisher's Warehouse
Books and magazines at a discount (varies by publisher).

Puddle Jumpers
Children's apparel from newborn to size 6 for girls, newborn to size 7 for boys. Full line of nursery accessories as well as other children's essentials at value prices.

Rack Room Shoes
Takes the "pinch" out of buying shoes by offering fashion footwear at affordable prices and the best in first-quality, name-brand styles like Aigner, Sam and Libby, Rockport, Florsheim, Sebago, Nike, and Reebok. The Rack Room is a family shoe store and has everything for men, women, and children, including an extensive stock of athletic shoes—all by famous makers at low prices—and a great selection of handbags, garments, and accessories.

Rawlings Sporting Goods

Baseball, basketball, and football uniforms and equipment at prices 20 to 40 percent off retail. Gifts and accessories, too.

Reader's Outlet

Enjoy a literary (shopper's) license with values from 25 to 70 percent off retail prices on reading material.

Reading Shoe

Exclusive Bass outlet with styles for men, women, and children. Savings of 20 to 50 percent off retail prices.

Reebok

Save 20 to 50 percent off suggested retail prices on all Reebok, Rockport, and Frye footwear, apparel, and accessories for men, women, and children.

Reeves Discount Outlet

Famous-label rainwear in both lined and unlined coats. Merchandise also includes golf jackets, hats, sweats, and sweater sets for men, women, and children. Expect at least a 50 percent discount. Sizes range from 36–54 regular and long (men); 4–24 regular and petite (women); 6 months to size 16 (children). Exchanges only, no refunds. Layaway plan: 20 percent down with payoff in ninety days.

Regal Ware

Factory-direct housewares featuring 30 to 70 percent savings on range-top cookware, portable kitchen appliances, and microwave ovenware. Good values on seconds, closeouts, and overruns as available.

Ribbon Outlet

Factory-direct savings on more than twenty-five hundred varieties of first-quality ribbons and trims. Cut your own "by the yard," or choose precut lengths or entire spools in bulk. Also offered are distinctively finished handcrafted gift items, selected craft supplies, and novelty and seasonal items. Personnel are knowledgeable about home sewing and crafts work. Savings of 20 to 50 percent off retail prices.

Rolane

Famous brand names at 30 to 50 percent below comparable retail prices. Ladies' apparel: dresses, coordinates, blouses, casual wear, lingerie, sheer hosiery, socks, and shoes. Men's apparel: casual wear, dress shirts, dress pants, shoes, ties, belts, underwear, socks. Accessories: handbags, wallets, luggage, briefcases. Children's socks. Direct-mail catalog available. Request forms available at each store or write to No Nonsense & More, P.O. Box 26095, Greensboro, NC 27420–6095. Sizes: ladies' apparel—coordinate and dress sizes 6–24; men's apparel—small, medium, large, X-large; sheer hosiery—all average sizes plus petite, tall, and queen sizes; socks—all men's, ladies', children's, and toddler sizes; shoes—men's 8–12, ladies' varies. All merchandise backed by 100 percent satisfaction guarantee. Extra selections may be ordered from sheer-hosiery catalog. Special discounts offered to senior citizens and members of the military.

Ropers Clothing

Regular sizes as well as big and tall. Name brands, Levi's, Roper western shirts, Wrangler-Brush Popper, Sansabelt jeans, Outback-Oil Duster, Flying Scotsman, Cotton Club, and nylon jogging suits, all at value prices.

Royal Doulton

Save from 20 to 70 percent on retail prices of Royal Doulton dinnerware, crystal, giftware, nurseryware, and figurines. In addition, save on select overstocks and on discontinued and special imports. UPS shipping.

Royal Robbins

Classic, stylish casual clothing for men and women, based on heritage of great outdoors.

Ruff Hewn

Men's and women's sportswear that offers rugged comfort for every occasion. Everyday savings of 35 to 50 percent or more. Sportswear items are geared for a comfortable, active life-style and for designer appeal.

Russell Mills, Russell Factory Store

Everything half price . . . every day. Sportswear, activewear, and leisure garments—T-shirts, fleecewear, sweatshirts, sweatpants, jackets, shorts, pullovers, and more. Overruns, closeouts, irregulars, and discontinued items, direct from the manufacturer.

Ruthie's
Carries famous brands of ladies' sportswear, dresses, and accessories discounted 50 to 80 percent.

Sabatier Cutlery
Imported French knives, stainless steel platters, and accessories, china, plus other delights from France (Limoge boxes, too). Discounts vary by product.

Samsonite
Source for everyday savings of up to 60 percent on Samsonite and Lark production samples and overstocked and discontinued items.

S & K Menswear
Discounted men's traditional clothing. Two thousand suits and sport coats from designer to classic, and only the finest quality. Features forty-eight brands, including Deansgate suits and sport coats. Also carries slacks, shirts, ties, and accessories. Sizes X-long in suits; sport coats up to size 50; big and tall dress shirts. The store buys from manufacturers, Bloomingdale's, and Lord and Taylor.

SBX
Ladies' and men's clothing at 25 to 70 percent off regular retail prices.

Scent Saver
Discounts on cosmetics, fragrances, gift sets, and accessories for men and women. The store carries fourteen fragrances produced by Scent Saver, plus other industry cosmetics and fragrances.

Seasons
Contemporary knitwear in solids and prints, plus accessories and jewelry. Discounts vary, but there is a 20 percent base. Sales are a daily constant.

Sequins Originals
Beaded gowns and dresses plus other coordinate outfits at a discount.

Sergio Valente
Fashions for men and women, including acid- and stone-washed jeans for both. Men will find values on Sergio Valente, Bugle Boy, and Union Bay; women, on Sergio Valente, Bugle Boy, Union Bay, Jenajer, Camp Beverly Hills, Miss Erika, Traffic, and California Ivy.

Ship 'n Shore
Values on these name-brand blouses.

Shoe Show
Twenty-five to 70 percent off regular retail prices on shoes for the entire family.

Shoe Store for Less
Family values at 25 to 70 percent off regular retail prices.

Shoe Strings
Save 20 to 60 percent off regular retail prices on name-brand women's and men's shoes, including Aigner, Proxy, Enzo, and Caressa.

Silkworm
Silk flowers, plants, and gifts of all kinds, plus glass, brass, and custom floral arrangements, as well as coral, candles, and soaps. Save 20 to 40 percent or more. Ships anywhere.

Smithy's Gifts and Lingerie
Value-oriented gifts for every occasion.

Sneakee Feet
"Sneak" something off the price of athletic shoes for the whole family. Selected styles from top names like Puma, Nike, Reebok, and Adidas. Save on selected athletic apparel, leisure wear, and sporting goods.

Socks Galore and More
More than sixty thousand pairs of socks—dress socks, sport socks,

tubes, and knee-highs for men, women, teens, and children. Designer fashions and basic styles; Anne Klein, Christian Dior, Camp, and more. All at savings of 40 to 70 percent.

Sound Junction
Tape, compact discs, videos, LPs, and accessories, from the latest hits to the greatest oldies at 10 to 75 percent off. Rock, country, big band, gospel, classical, and more.

South Carolina Sportswear
Twenty-five to 70 percent off regular retail prices on all types of sporting apparel.

Southern Charm
Unique handcrafted treasures with prices that are a real find. Vintage collectibles, fabric and lace original creations, and quality handcrafted pine furniture reproductions. Thirty to 60 percent off retail prices.

Sox Shoppe
Just what the name implies, at 25 to 70 percent off regular retail prices.

Sports Outlet
Nike, Reebok, New Balance, Converse, K-Swiss, Tretorn, Rockport, Asics, and more. Savings up to 70 percent.

Sports Page
Choose from major brands of discounted athletic shoes for the entire family, and select your favorite team for apparel and gifts from the NFL, NBA, MLB, NHL, and NCAA.

Sportswear Depot
Substantial savings on sportswear.

Sports Wearhouse
Excellent values on Chalkline, the store's exclusive product.

Springmaid/Wamsutta
Linens made in America from 100 percent cotton and cotton/polyester

blends in a variety of patterns and solid colors. Recognized values for bed, bath, and kitchen. Percale sheets, bedspreads, comforters, bed accessories, window treatments, pillows, towels, and more. Shipping available.

Stanly Knitting Mill
Save 30 to 70 percent every day on SK Sport activewear. Irregulars and first-quality sold. Jeans, lingerie, and accessories. Headwear for the entire family.

Starbaby
Designer apparel for children in comfortable 100 percent cotton. Sizes newborn to 7.

Starter
Manufacturer of authentic licensed sports apparel and accessories of the NFL, MLB, NHL, NBA, and NCAA.

Stone Mountain Handbags
Save 20 to 50 percent on first-quality leather and nonleather Stone Mountain handbags. Men's and women's leather accessories also available.

Strasburg Lace
French, hand-sewn apparel for girls ages six months to fourteen years, and little boys, sizes 6 months to 4T, at a discount.

Sunglass World
Save up to 25 percent on national brands including Ray-Ban, Serengeti, Eyescreens, Porsche, and more.

Sun Shades 501, Ltd.
Values on Ray-Ban sunglasses.

Sunspecs Sunglass Superstore
Famous brand-name sunglasses and eyeglass frames, including Ray-Ban, Serengeti, Bolle, Vaumet, and Miro at discount prices. Many styles and prices.

Swank
Discounts on garment and tote bags, portfolios, attachés, wallets, and the like. Jewelry lines include Swank, Pierre Cardin, Alexander Julien, L'Aiglon, Aigner, Anne Klein, 90 Park, and Biagi. Extensive selections. Up to 70 percent off manufacturer's listed price.

Sweater Shops
Women's sweaters, shirts, and warm-ups. Discounted name brands include California Ivy, College Point, Billy Jo, Cyn Les, Colter Bay, Crystal, D.D. Sloan, Eddie Dassin, Lady Arrow, Knit Works, Le Choice, Northern Isles, Western Connection, and Here's a Hug. Carries extra-large sweaters and shirts in sizes 36–46. Also carries costume jewelry.

Sweatshirt Co.
Mix and match styles, colors, and sizes for all, including big and tall men and women, at savings up to 70 percent.

Tanner
Classic women's clothing, from casual to elegant, all at factory-direct savings. Brands include Tanner, Tanner Sport, and DK Gold. Save 30 to 75 percent off suggested retail.

Tie One On
Twenty-five to 40 percent off regular retail prices on fashion neckwear.

Today's Child
Contemporary clothing for boys and girls. Discounts vary by manufacturer.

Top of the Line Fragrances and Cosmetics
An extensive selection and savings on all types of cosmetics. More than fifty name brands are carried by this outlet, including designer fragrances for women and men by Elizabeth Arden, Lilli Treselle, and more. Savings up to 70 percent.

Totes
Save up to 70 percent on Totes and associated brands: umbrellas, raincoats, luggage, and headwear for men and women. The outlet features

overstocks, closeouts, discontinued styles and colors, and some irregulars. Save up to 25 percent additional on national-brand sunglasses including Ray-Ban, Serengeti, Carerra, and Gatorz.

Toy Liquidators
Thousands of brand-name toys at less than manufacturer's original wholesale prices, with new merchandise arriving daily. Carries overstocks, package changes, and discontinued items in such major lines as Playskool, Fisher-Price, Hasbro, Tonka, and Mattel. Discounts of up to 75 percent off or more.

Toy Outlet
Fun and games at 25 to 70 percent off regular retail prices.

Toys Unlimited
Featuring thousands of nationally advertised, top-quality, name-brand toys at savings up to 75 percent off retail. New goods arrive daily.

Toy Town
Seventy percent savings on name-brand toys.

Trader Kids
Children's wear at 25 to 70 percent off regular retail prices.

Treasure Chest
Brand-name and novelty knives by Buck, Case, Kissing Crane, and Bokers. Also carries personalized license tags, sweatshirts, T-shirts, transfers, and more, all at 25 to 50 percent off suggested retail prices.

Tropic Art
A full-service art gallery offering custom framing and decorative gifts and accessories. Featured are fine-art watercolors and prints by Sina and Jim Gerard Holehouse, as well as a complete selection of art posters, reproductions, and limited-edition prints.

Uncommon Scents
Discounts on perfume, potpourri, scented candles, soap, and everything else that smells good.

Uniform/Lingerie Connection
Women's uniforms, lingerie, and duty shoes. Discounted name brands include Nursemates and Great Stride by Nike in shoes; White Swan, Barco, Crest, and Bob Evans in uniforms; and Lily of France and Gilead in lingerie. A large selection of bras; all sizes in uniforms.

Unisa
First-quality ladies' footwear, handbags, and accessories. Save 30 to 70 percent.

United Apparel, Ltd.
Men's and women's brand-name clothing for less.

U.S. Textile Outlet
Save 60 to 70 percent off manufacturer's suggested retail on bedspreads, comforters, curtains, drapes, and more.

Van Heusen, Phillips Van Heusen
"The Van Heusen shirt—for a man to buy and a woman to borrow." Men's shirts, ties, belts, and casual wear. First-quality, in-season fashion merchandise for men and women, including Lady Van Heusen and designer-brand apparel. Buy direct from the manufacturer and save 25 to 60 percent off suggested retail prices on every item every day. A "no question" return policy guarantees satisfaction.

Vanity Fair, VF Factory Outlet
Vanity Fair, Lee, Health-Tex, Jantzen, JanSport, and Lollipop are just a few of the nationally famous brand names you'll find at this outlet. From socks to jeans, lingerie to dresses, shirts to jackets, ties to outerwear, the extensive racks are sure to yield savings galore, always 50 percent off lowest ticketed price.

Variety Crafts
More than three thousand handmade items to please the purse.

Victoria Creations
Fashion jewelry by Lisner, Richelieu, Givenchy, and others. Save 20 to 50 percent off retail prices.

Village Books
Thousands of titles—fiction, nonfiction, paperback, and hardback. Discounts vary by publisher.

Village Boutique
Unique jewelry and gifts for less.

Village Frame Shop
Frames at 30 to 60 percent off regular retail prices.

Village Furniture House
Name-brand furnishings at North Carolina prices. Discounts vary by brand.

Villeroy & Boch
China and crystal factory outlet (seconds and first-quality discontinued patterns).

Virginia's
Discounts on fine-quality merchandise, featuring all-occasion dresses, suits, lingerie, and accessories.

Vision Land
Thousands of eyeglass frames at discount prices.

Waccamaw Pottery
The company's advertising promises to make each customer a "low price winner," with a guarantee of discounted prices on large quantities of merchandise; if customers find a lower price (at another outlet) on an identical piece of merchandise carried through Waccamaw, the management promises to beat the price. Selections of merchandise include dinnerware, housewares, wicker, dried and silk flowers, flower arrangements, and giftware all discounted as much as 80 percent off regular department-store prices. Fine quality and superior values on name-brand merchandise: Look for Mikasa, Libbey, Rubbermaid, Corning, Anchor-Hocking, and others.

Wallet Works
Factory owned and operated, selling first-quality men's and women's

leather billfolds, accessories, luggage, handbags, briefcases, and travel gifts, all at 25 to 70 percent savings below suggested retail prices.

Walnut Bowls/Chicago Cutlery
Case knives, Chicago Cutlery, picture frames and mats, art prints, walnut items.

Warnaco
Save up to 60 percent off men's fashions and ladies' intimate apparel. Famous labels include Christian Dior, Hathaway, Ralph Lauren, Jack Nicklaus, Olga, and Warner's.

Welcome Home
Uniquely crafted decorative accessories, potpourri, and gifts for every occasion at 20 to 50 percent below retail prices.

WEMCO/Wembley Factory Store
World's largest tie manufacturer offers more than 10,000 name-brand neckties of all looks to choose from at savings from 50 to 80 percent. Specialty-store quality men's casual apparel at savings from 40 to 60 percent.

West Point Pepperell Bed, Bath and Linens Factory Outlet
Offers one of the South's largest selections of famous-label products, featuring first-quality items, selected irregulars, and factory closeouts of such internationally known brands as Martex and Lady Pepperell sheets and towels, Cabin Crafts rugs and carpets, and Vellux miracle blankets, all direct from the mills. Stores also have selections of gift and novelty items, as well as accessories for bed and bath. Featured are Ladies Planning Room, The Shirt Rack, The World of Floor Fashions, The Bedding Inn, The Pillow Place, The Great Bath Shop, Martex Towel Country, The Linen Korner, The Atelier Shop, and Sheet Fashions. Discounts vary from manufacturer to manufacturer. Mailing list maintained by sign register. Special coupons sent to mailing list members. In-store special orders are available. Refund or exchange with sales receipt.

Westport
Famous-label fashions . . . factory to you! Prices on branded goods 20 to

50 percent less than department-store prices. Shop from a beautiful collection of suits, dresses, sportswear, and separates in sizes 4–14. No sale is ever final.

Whims
Ladies' jewelry (Sarah Coventry brand) at generous discounts up to 70 percent off manufacturer's retail prices. Factory owned.

Windsor Shirt
Quality dress shirts and sportswear for men at 25 to 40 percent off regular retail prices.

Wolf Camera & Video
An excellent selection of brand-name equipment and accessories. Superior-quality, one-hour film developing features Wolfpro Big prints for bigger and brighter pictures with true-to-life color.

Yes Brazil
Featuring brand-name electronics, watches, sunglasses, perfumes, toys, and skateboards.

Young Generations
A factory outlet that features the world-famous products of this quality manufacturer. Offers a complete selection of Ruth and Carolina girls' dresses (toddler to size 14) and Picture Me fashion-forward dresses and sportswear for young juniors/teens. All prices, including those for first-quality items and slight irregulars, are at true factory discounts, 25 to 70 percent off regular retail prices.

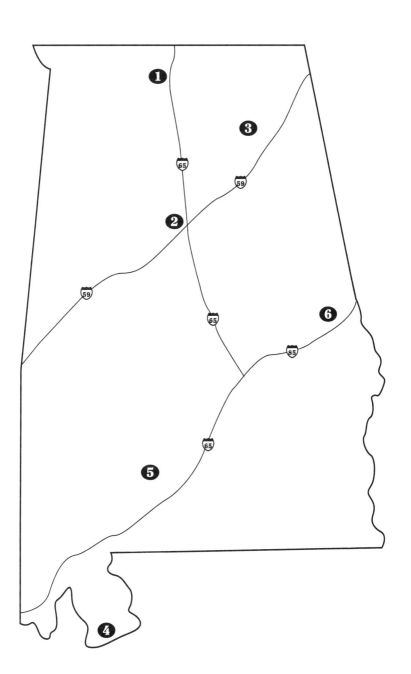

Alabama

Numbers at the left of this legend correspond to the numbers on the accompanying map. The number to the right of each city's or town's name is the page number on which that municipality's outlets first appear in this book.

1. Athens, 58
2. Birmingham, 58
3. Boaz, 59
4. Foley, 65
5. Monroeville, 67
6. Opelika, 68

Athens

Acme Boot Company, Inc.
1699 Highway 72, East

Directions: Take I–65 to Huntsville, exit 351. Outlet is ½ mile on the left.
Phone: (615) 552–2000, ext. 267
Hours: 9:00 A.M.–8:00 P.M., Monday–Saturday; 11:00 A.M.–6:00 P.M., Sunday. *Thanksgiving–Christmas:* 9:00 A.M.–9:00 P.M., Monday–Saturday; 11:00 A.M.–7:00 P.M., Sunday.
Credit Cards: American Express, Discover, MasterCard, Visa
Personal Checks: Yes, with valid driver's license or other identification
Food: Yes, in vicinity
Bus Tours: Yes; advance notice appreciated
Notes or Attractions: NASA Space and Rocket Center is twenty-five minutes away.

Birmingham

Barry Manufacturing Company
1701 Third Avenue, West

Directions: Take I–59 South, Arkadelphia exit. Turn left, pass College, and turn right onto Third Avenue.
Phone: (205) 781–1901
Hours: 9:00 A.M.–7:00 P.M., Monday–Friday; 9:00 A.M.–6:00 P.M., Saturday; 12:30 P.M.–5:00 P.M., Sunday
Credit Cards: American Express, Discover, MasterCard, Visa
Personal Checks: Yes
Food: Fast-food establishments in the immediate vicinity
Bus Tours: Yes

Boaz

Special Note: As mentioned in the Introduction, the city of Boaz has proclaimed itself the "Outlet Capital of the South." As this book went to press, Boaz had more than 130 famous-brand factory outlets, with more being planned. Boaz has been listed as "one of the top three centers for outlet shopping in the United States," with the two top anchor stores in the outlet business—Vanity Fair and West Point Pepperell. Stevens Outlet is also located in Boaz.

To reach Boaz: From I–59, exit 183 at Attalla, Alabama; end of ramp, turn left on U.S. Highway 431 North to Boaz. To receive a map and other current information, write Boaz Outlet Bulletin, P.O. Box 564, Boaz, Alabama 35957, or call the Chamber of Commerce at (205) 593–8154.

Boaz Outlet Center
425 McClesky Street

Directions: Take Highway 168 west (Mill Street) or Billy B. Dyar Boulevard off U.S. Highway 431. The center is adjacent to Vanity Fair Factory Outlet Mall.
Phone: (205) 593–9306
Hours: 9:00 A.M.–9:00 P.M., Monday–Saturday; 12:30–5:30 P.M., Sunday
Outlets:
Aileen
Athlete's Foot
Bass Shoes
Bon Worth
Book Factory
Boot Factory
Brass Factory
Burlington Brands
Capezio
Carter's
Childcraft
Corning Revere
Donnkenny
Ducks Unlimited
Euro Collections/Bleyle
Everything's A Dollar
Farah

Fieldcrest/Cannon
Fruit of the Loom
Full Size Fashions
Hush Puppies
Izod
Jaymar
Jerzees
Jockey
Jonathan Logan
Judy Bond Blouses
Kitchen Collection
Knife Factory
Leather Loft
L'eggs/Hanes/Bali
Libbey Glass
Maidenform
Naturalizer
$9.99 Stockroom/Caper's
Oneida
Pfaltzgraff
Polly Flinders
Rack Room Shoes
Ribbon Outlet
Royal Doulton
SBX
Socks Galore and More
Sports Wearhouse
Swank
Tie One On
Today's Child
Top of the Line Fragrances and Cosmetics
Toy Liquidators
Van Heusen
Wallet Works
Welcome Home
WEMCO
West Point Pepperell
Westport

> Due to corporate restrictions as outlined by this outlet mall, the publisher has been unable to provide profiles on the following outlets. These outlets have also been deleted from the indexes.

Creekwood
East of Italy Jewelry
Famous Brands
Garment District
Missy Sportswear Plus
Paragon Decor
Reading China and Glass
Sewell Factory Store
Credit Cards: Most stores accept American Express, Discover, MasterCard, and Visa
Personal Checks: Yes, with proper identification
Food: Mrs. Tupper's Family Buffet and various fast-food establishments
Bus Tours: Yes. Call in advance to schedule. A complete "Group Tour Policy" and additional information are available by calling (205) 593–9306. Convenient bus parking, bus driver's lounge, and easy access to all factory outlets makes a trip to this outlet center a pleasure!
Notes or Attractions: Annual Harvest Festival in October in Boaz; Lake Guntersville, 15 miles north; Noccalula Falls, 20 miles south. Closeout house located on-site has tenants who rotate weekly with special or closeout merchandise.

Fashion Outlets
501 Elizabeth Street

Directions: Take Highway 168 west (or Billy B. Dyar Boulevard) off U.S. Highway 431.
Phone: (205) 593–1199
Hours: *January–February:* 9:00 A.M.–6:00 P.M., Monday–Thursday; 9:00 A.M.–9:00 P.M., Friday–Saturday; 12:30–5:30 P.M., Sunday. *March–June:* 9:00 A.M.–8:00 P.M., Monday–Thursday; 9:00 A.M.–9:00 P.M., Friday–Saturday; 12:30–5:30 P.M., Sunday. *July–December:* 9:00 A.M.–9:00 P.M., Monday–Saturday; 12:00–5:00 P.M., Sunday.

Outlets:
Anne Klein
Arrow Factory Store
Bible Outlet
Book Warehouse
Boston Trader Kids
Clothestime
Collector's Gallery
Dollartime
Dress Barn
Dress Barn Woman
Duck Head
Eagle's Eye
Etienne Aigner
Factory Connection
Fila
Gold Market
Gold Toe
J. Crew
J. H. Collectibles
Johnston & Murphy
Jones New York
L & S Shoes
Leathers by Mullins
Levi's
London Fog
Nettle Creek
Nike
Nilani
Perfumania
Polo
Ruthie's
S & K Menswear
Strasburg Lace
Totes/Sunglass World
Toy Town
Credit Cards: Most stores accept American Express, Discover, Visa, and MasterCard.

Personal Checks: Yes, with proper identification
ATM: Nearby
Food: Yes

Tanger Factory Outlet Center
(Under the Red Roof)
214 South McClesky

Directions: From I–59, exit 183, left on U.S. Highway 431; north to Boaz. Once you are on Billy B. Dyar Boulevard, look for the Red Roof.
Phone: (205) 593–9038
Hours: *January–February:* 9:00 A.M.–6:00 P.M., Monday–Wednesday; 9:00 A.M.–9:00 P.M., Thursday–Saturday; 12:00–6:00 P.M., Sunday. *March–December:* 9:00 A.M.–9:00 P.M., Monday–Saturday; 12:00–6:00 P.M., Sunday.
Outlets:
Allen Edmonds
Barbizon Lingerie
Bass Shoes
Bugle Boy
Cape Isle Knitters
Eddie Bauer
Geoffrey Beene
Gorham
Leslie Fay
Liz Claiborne
Mikasa
OshKosh B'Gosh (The Genuine Article)
Reebok
Samsonite
Unisa
Van Heusen
Credit Cards: American Express, Discover, MasterCard, Visa
Personal Checks: Yes, with two forms of identification
Additional Savings: Savings of 30 to 70 percent year-round; sidewalk sales in April and the first weekend in October

Food: Cafeteria across the street; a deli one block away; fast-food places all along U.S. Highway 431

Bus Tours: Yes. The center offers both the bus driver and the tour guide a $15 check, free pair of Reebok tennis shoes, or free pair of Bugle Boy Jeans.

Notes or Attractions: NASA Space and Rocket Center is about forty-five minutes away; Lake Guntersville State Park is about twenty minutes away.

Vanity Fair Factory Outlet Mall
East Mill Avenue and Lackey Street

Directions: From I–59, exit onto U.S. Highway 431; head north to Boaz. Turn left on Billy B. Dyar Boulevard and continue about 1.5 miles. The mall is adjacent to the Boaz Outlet Center.

Phone: (205) 593–2930

Hours: *January–February:* 9:00 A.M.–7:00 P.M., Monday–Thursday; 9:00 A.M.–9:00 P.M., Friday–Saturday; 12:00–5:00 P.M., Sunday. *March–June:* 9:00 A.M.–8:00 P.M., Monday–Thursday; 9:00 A.M.–9:00 P.M., Friday–Saturday; 12:00–5:30 P.M., Sunday. *July–December:* 9:00 A.M.–8:00 P.M., Monday–Thursday; 9:00 A.M.–9:00 P.M., Friday; 8:00 A.M.–9:00 P.M., Saturday; 12:00–5:30 P.M., Sunday.

Outlets:
American Tourister
Banister Shoes
Black & Decker
Evan-Picone
Jewelry Outlet
Paper Factory
Prestige Fragrance
Vanity Fair, VF Factory Outlet

Credit Cards: Discover, MasterCard, Visa

Personal Checks: Yes, with photo driver's license

ATM: Yes, at local banks nearby

Food: Deli sandwiches and pizza available within the complex

Bus Tours: Call ahead for special shopping and parking instructions.
Alternate Transportation: Tram runs daily, making rounds through the area about every forty-five minutes.
Notes or Attractions: Lake Guntersville State Park; in January and February, eagle-watching parties

Foley

King Clock Company
2600 South McKenzie Street

Directions: I–10 exit from Loxley to Highway 59 South, 18 miles down the road on right, across from the Riviera Centre Mall
Phone: (205) 943–5115
Hours: 9:00 A.M.–5:00 P.M., Monday–Saturday
Credit Cards: American Express, Discover, MasterCard, Visa
Personal Checks: Yes, with two identifications
Food: Across the street
Bus Tours: Yes
Notes or Attractions: Located ten minutes from the beach at Gulf Shores, Alabama

Riviera Centre Factory Stores
2601 South McKenzie Street

Directions: From the north, take I–65 south, exit at Highway 59, exit 37 (Gulf Shores Parkway), and head south (approximately 45 miles). From the west, take I–10 east, exit at Spanish Fort (exit 44), and follow Highway 98 east to Highway 59; turn south onto Route 50 (approximately 2 miles). From the east, take I–10 west to Highway 59 (exit 44) South (approximately 22 miles).
Phone: (205) 943–8888 or (800) 5–CENTRE (528–6873)
Hours: 9:00 A.M.–9:00 P.M., Monday–Saturday; 10:00 A.M.–6:00 P.M., Sunday (seasonal hours may vary)

Outlets:

Adolfo II
Adrienne Vittadini
Aileen
American Tourister
Arrow Factory Store
Aureus
Banister Shoes
Bass Shoes
Bon Worth
Book Factory
Boot Factory
Boston Trader Kids
Boston Traders
Bruce Alan Bags
Bugle Boy
Burlington Brands
Calvin Klein
Capezio
Carter's
Childcraft
Coach
Colours
Corning Revere
Country Road Australia
Crazy Horse
Dansk
Danskin
Dexter Shoes
Duck Head
Eagle's Eye
Eagle's Eye Kids
Ellen Tracy
Etienne Aigner
Evan-Picone
Famous Brands Housewares
Geoffrey Beene
Gilligan & O'Malley

Guess?
harvé benard
I.B. Diffusion
J. Crew
Jerzees
Jewel Mart, USA
Johnston & Murphy
Jones New York
Judy Bond Blouses
Kitchen Collection
Leather Loft
L'eggs/Hanes/Bali
Leslie Fay
Levi's
Liz Claiborne
Magnavox
Maidenform
Manhattan
Mikasa
Multiples
Nautica
9 West
Olga/Warner's
Oneida
OshKosh B'Gosh (The Genuine
    Article)
Outlet Marketplace
Paper Factory
Patchington
Perfumania
Pfaltzgraff
Polly Flinders
Polo/Ralph Lauren
Prestige Fragrance
Rawlings Sporting Goods
Reebok
Ribbon Outlet
Ruff Hewn

Socks Galore
Starter
Strasburg Lace
Toys Unlimited
Van Heusen

Wallet Works
Welcome Home
WEMCO
West Point Pepperell
Westport

Credit Cards: Varies from store to store. Most factory stores accept major credit cards (American Express, Discover, MasterCard, and Visa).
Personal Checks: In most stores, with identification
Food: Food court with numerous selections
Bus Tours: Yes. Bus parking in rear of center. Coupon books and shopping bags for groups. Free meals for tour guides and drivers.
Notes or Attractions: Tourist area. Nine miles of Gulf Shore beaches, which boast 32 miles of sugar-white beaches, water parks, zoo, golfing, tennis, and eight marinas. Gulf State Park, Bon Secour Wildlife Refuge, and historic Fort Morgan.

Monroeville

Vanity Fair Outlet
Drewry Road

Directions: Take I–65 to Evergreen/Monroeville exit. Proceed west on Highway 84 to Highway 21 north. Bear right onto Highway 21 bypass, right onto Roberts Drive to Vanity Fair Outlet.
Phone: (205) 575–2330
Hours: *January–September:* 9:00 A.M.–6:00 P.M., Monday–Saturday; 12:00–5:30 P.M., Sunday. *October–December:* 9:00 A.M.–6:00 P.M., Monday–Thursday; 9:00 A.M.–8:00 P.M., Friday–Saturday; 12:00–5:30 P.M., Sunday.
Credit Cards: Discover, MasterCard, Visa
Personal Checks: Yes, with proper identification (driver's license, social security card, or military identification)
Food: Fast food in the immediate area
Bus Tours: Bus parking is available. Upon registration, shopping bags with discount coupons will be given to passengers. Drivers also receive a gift certificate.

Alternate Transportation: VF Factory Outlet offers free transportation to and from the Monroe County Airport.

Notes or Attractions: In downtown Monroeville sits the historic Monroe County Courthouse, which houses the Monroe County Heritage Museum. The one-act play *To Kill a Mockingbird* is presented seasonally in the old courtroom of the Monroe County Courthouse. The Alabama River is located 15 miles away and provides excellent recreational boating, fishing, and camping.

Opelika

USA Factory Stores
1220 Fox Run Parkway

Directions: I–85, exit 62 to U.S. Highway 431 North
Phone: (205) 749–0561
Hours: 9:00 A.M.–9:00 P.M., Monday–Saturday; 12:00–6:00 P.M., Sunday (Central Standard Time)
Outlets:
Arrow Factory Store
Banister Shoes
Barbizon Lingerie
Bass Shoes
Bugle Boy
Carolina Clock & Rug
Corning Revere
Duck Head
Famous Brands Housewares
Fragrance Cove
Hush Puppies
Le Creuset
L'eggs/Hanes/Bali
Libbey Glass Factory Outlet
M.C. Sox
Paper Factory
Publisher's Book Outlet/Card Barn

Ribbon Outlet
Ship 'n Shore
Springmaid/Wamsutta
Toy Liquidators
Van Heusen
Welcome Home
Westport

Credit Cards: MasterCard, Visa; each store has its own credit-card policy; some take American Express

Personal Checks: Yes, with two forms of identification

Additional Savings: Promotional calendar changes: February, April, June, August, October, November, and December

Food: Food court area, plus restaurants within immediate vicinity

Bus Tours: Yes, check in at Center Office. Discount coupon books available for groups. Driver's lounge has a television.

Notes or Attractions: Callaway Gardens, Georgia, 40 miles; Warm Springs, Georgia, with Little White House, 45 miles; Auburn University, 10 miles; 54-hole "Links on the Lake" (Robert Trent Jones–designed golf course)

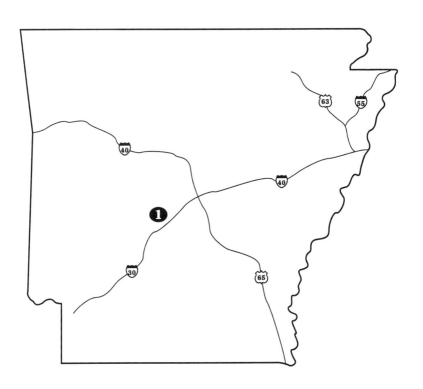

Arkansas

The number at the left of this legend corresponds to the number on the accompanying map. The number to the right of the city's name is the page number on which that municipality's outlets first appear in this book.

1. Hot Springs, 72

Hot Springs

Hot Springs Factory Outlet Stores
4332 Central Avenue

Directions: Take Highway 7 South; the store is 3 miles south of Oaklawn Raceway.
Phone: (501) 525–0888
Hours: 10:00 A.M.–9:00 P.M., Monday–Saturday; 12:00–6:00 P.M., Sunday

Outlets:
Aileen
Bon Worth
Book Warehouse
Bugle Boy
Cape Isle Knitters
Capezio
Corning Revere
Famous Footwear
Fieldcrest/Cannon
Florsheim Shoe
Geoffrey Beene
Jonathan Logan
Judy Bond Blouses
Kitchen Collection
Leather Loft
No Nonsense & More
Paper Factory
Polly Flinders
Reading Shoe Outlet
Ribbon Outlet
Sequins Originals
Socks Galore and More
Top of the Line Fragrances and Cosmetics
Van Heusen
Victoria Creations
Welcome Home
Westport

Credit Cards: MasterCard and Visa in most stores

Personal Checks: In most stores, Arkansas checks are accepted with proper identification (Arkansas driver's license). A few stores accept out-of-state checks.

Additional Savings: After-Christmas Sale (around the week of January 7); July 4th Sale

Food: Restaurant and snack shop

Bus Tours: Check-in points: Leather Loft and the Aileen store. Customer appreciation booklets available, offering coupons to various stores for groups.

Notes or Attractions: This is the only factory outlet mall in the state of Arkansas—the next nearest outlet area is in Branson, Missouri. Hot Springs National Park is noted for its "hot springs" bathhouses; Oaklawn Raceway has thoroughbred horses; music shows and a family theme park (summer only); plus the Mid-America Museum, a hands-on science museum.

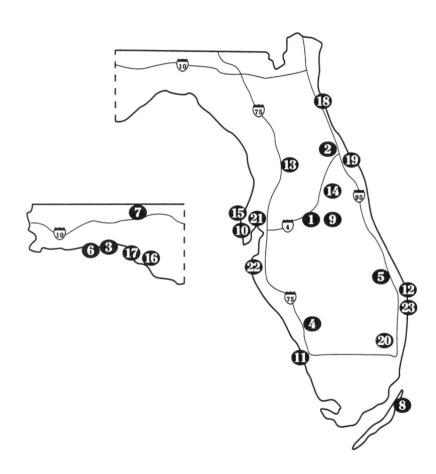

Florida

Numbers at the left of this legend correspond to the numbers on the accompanying map. The number to the right of each city's or town's name is the page number on which that municipality's outlets first appear in this book.

Davenport

Acme Boot Factory Outlet
4721 U.S. 27 North

Directions: Take I–4 to exit 23. Outlet is south about half a mile, next to Denny's restaurant.
Phone: (615) 552–2000, ext. 267
Hours: 9:00 A.M.–9:00 P.M., Monday–Sunday
Credit Cards: American Express, Discover, MasterCard, Visa
Personal Checks: Yes, with valid driver's license
Food: Yes, in vicinity
Bus Tours: Yes; advance notice appreciated
Notes or Attractions: Just minutes from Disney World, Sea World, and Cypress Gardens

Daytona Beach

Acme Boot Factory Outlet
2951 Volusia Avenue

Directions: From the north, take I–95 south to exit 87A (Highway 92 East); the outlet is a quarter mile on the right. From Orlando, take I–4 east to the Highway 92 exit; the outlet is 5 miles on the right.
Phone: (615) 552–2000, ext. 267
Hours: 9:00 A.M.–9:00 P.M., Monday through Saturday; 9:00 A.M.–6:00 P.M., Sunday
Credit Cards: American Express, Discover, MasterCard, Visa
Personal Checks: Yes, with valid driver's license or other identification
Food: Waffle House and Western Steer are within parking area. Within a quarter of a mile are Red Lobster and Howard Johnson's.
Bus Tours: Yes. Parking is available at the front of the store.
Notes or Attractions: Beach is ten minutes away; Marine Land is 30 miles north; jai alai; Kennel Club; Daytona 500 is only minutes away

Destin

Arrow
Silver Sands Factory Stores
5101 Highway 98 East

Directions: Highway 98 east from Pensacola, west from Panama City. Near Sandestin Resort in Destin. From I–10, take State Road 331 or Mid-Bay Bridge South.
Phone: (904) 654–9711
Hours: 10:00 A.M.–9:00 P.M., Monday–Saturday; 10:00 A.M.–6:00 P.M., Sunday
Credit Cards: MasterCard, Visa
Personal Checks: Yes
Food: Yes
Bus Tours: Yes
Notes or Attractions: Outlet mall is minutes away from Sandestin Beach Resort; beach access is across from mall. Pensacola is 60 miles away.

Dansk Factory Outlet
Silver Sands Factory Stores
5101 Highway 98 East, Suite 62

Directions: Highway 98 east from Pensacola, west from Panama City. Near Sandestin Resort in Destin. From I–10, take State Road 331 or Mid-Bay Bridge South.
Phone: (804) 654–0030
Hours: 10:00 A.M.–9:00 P.M., Monday–Saturday; 10:00 A.M.–6:00 P.M., Sunday
Credit Cards: MasterCard, Visa
Personal Checks: Yes, with driver's license if total is more than $150
ATM: Yes, a bank is across from the mall.
Food: Yes, a food court is on the premises.
Bus Tours: Yes, anywhere near tower. Prearrangements are helpful.
Notes or Attractions: Outlet mall is minutes away from Sandestin Beach Resort; beach access is across from mall. Pensacola is 60 miles away.

Ft. Myers

Sanibel Factory Stores
20350 Summerlin Road

Directions: From I–75, take exit 21 going west to Summerlin Road. Take a left, and the Sanibel Factory Stores will be on the right about 8 miles down the road.
Phone: (813) 454–1616
Hours: 10:00 A.M.–9:00 P.M., Monday–Saturday; 11:00 A.M.–6:00 P.M., Sunday; closed Easter, Thanksgiving, and Christmas
Outlets:
Aileen
American Tourister
Banister Shoes
Bass Shoes
Bon Worth
Book Warehouse
Bugle Boy
Cape Isle Knitters
Carter's
Corning Revere
Famous Brands Housewares
Famous Footwear
Farah
Full Size Fashions
Geoffrey Beene
Gitano
Kitchen Collection
Leather Loft
Le Creuset
L'eggs/Hanes/Bali
Lenox
Maidenform
Multiples
Oneida
Palm Beach
Paper Factory

Pfaltzgraff
Prestige Fragrance & Cosmetics, PFC Fragrance
Rawlings Sporting Goods
Reebok
Royal Doulton
Russell Mills, Russell Factory Store
Socks Galore and More
Stone Mountain Handbags
Swank
Totes
Toys Unlimited
Van Heusen
Wallet Works
Welcome Home
West Point Pepperell Bed, Bath, and Linens Factory Outlet
Credit Cards: Varies by store, but expect MasterCard and Visa
Personal Checks: Yes, accepted with a driver's license
Food: Restaurant is located at the northeast corner of the center.
Bus Tours: Yes. Call management office for guidelines.
Notes or Attractions: Ft. Myers Beach is ten minutes away; Sanibel Island is 3 miles west.

Ft. Pierce

Manufacturer's Outlet Center
2769 Peters Road

Directions: Intersection of I–95, exit 65, and the Florida Turnpike, exit 152 (state road 70), Ft. Pierce, Florida
Hours: 9:00 A.M.–8:00 P.M., Monday–Saturday; 11:00 A.M.–5:00 P.M., Sunday
Outlets:
Acme Boot
Adolfo II
Aileen
American Tourister

Banister Shoes
Bass Shoes
Bon Worth
Book Warehouse
Converse Shoe
Corning Revere
Dexter Shoes
Farberware, Inc.
Fieldcrest/Cannon
Fila
Full Size Fashions
Geoffrey Beene
Golf Outlet
Jonathan Logan
Judy Bond Blouses
Kitchen Collection
Langtry
Leather Loft
Levi's
London Fog
Manhattan
OskKosh B'Gosh (The Genuine Article)
Polly Flinders
Prestige Fragrance & Cosmetics, PFC Fragrance
Rack Room Shoes
Ribbon Outlet
Russell Mills, Russell Factory Store
Swank
Toys Unlimited
Van Heusen
Vision Land
Wallet Works
Welcome Home
Westport
Credit Cards: American Express, Discover, MasterCard, Visa
Personal Checks: Yes
ATM: Yes, within 1 mile
Food: Yes, on-site and within area

Bus Tours: Yes
Notes or Attractions: Jai alai nearby; surrounded by famous Indian River Citrus areas. Beaches are ten minutes away. Major crossover for interstate and turnpike travelers.

Ft. Walton Beach

Manufacturer's Outlet Center
127 and 255 Highway 98

Directions: Located on Highway 98, downtown Ft. Walton Beach
Phone: Not available to public
Hours: *Summer:* 9:00 A.M.–9:00 P.M., Monday–Saturday; 11:00 A.M.–6:00 P.M., Sunday. *Winter:* 10:00 A.M.–9:00 P.M., Monday–Saturday; 11:00 A.M.–5:00 P.M., Sunday.
Credit Cards: American Express, Discover, MasterCard, Visa
Outlets:
Aileen
Bass Apparel
Bass Shoes
Bon Worth
Cape Isle Knitters
Capezio
Carter's
Converse Shoe
Corning Revere
Fieldcrest/Cannon
Geoffrey Beene
Jerzees
Jockey
Judy Bond Blouses
Kitchen Collection
L'eggs/Hanes/Bali
Levi's
Polly Flinders
Russell Factory Store

Swank
Van Heusen
Wallet Works
Westport
Personal Checks: Yes
Food: In the immediate area
Bus Tours: Yes
Alternate Transportation: Free trolley service around the mall
Notes or Attractions: Sugar-white beaches are one block away. Near amusement parks, Gulfarium, restaurants, Indian Temple Mound Museum, Focus Center (hands-on museum). Air Force Armament Museum is ten minutes away.

Graceville

Factory Stores of America
302 West Prim Avenue

Directions: I–10 to exit 18, north on Highway 77, 12 miles to Graceville
Phone: (800) 554–7163
Hours: 9:00 A.M.–7:00 P.M., Monday–Thursday; 9:00 A.M.–8:00 P.M., Friday–Saturday; 12:00–5:30 P.M., Sunday
Outlets:
Banister Shoes
Black & Decker
Bon Worth
Corning Revere
Easy Spirit & Co.
Jewelry Outlet
Ocean Galleries
Paper Factory
Prestige Fragrance & Cosmetics, PFC Fragrance
Van Heusen
Vanity Fair, VF Factory Outlet
Credit Cards: Most major companies; varies by store

Personal Checks: Yes, for the amount of purchase and with proper identification
Food: Pizza parlor and deli
Bus Tours: Yes, with coupons
Notes or Attractions: On-site events and entertainment on various weekends

VF Factory Outlet Mall
Highway 77 South and West Prim Avenue

Directions: *From Dothan:* Take Highway 231 South to Highway 2 West. At Graceville, go south on Highway 77; look for sign. *From Panama City:* Take Highway 77 North toward Graceville; look for sign. *From Valdosta:* Take Highway 84 West to Highway 319 South, Highway 319 to I–10 West exit 18, north on Highway 77 toward Graceville; look for sign. *From Tallahassee:* Take exit 18 west off I–10, north on Highway 77 toward Graceville; look for sign.
Phone: (904) 263–3207
Hours: *January–September:* 9:00 A.M.–6:00 P.M., Monday–Thursday; 9:00 A.M.–8:00 P.M., Friday–Saturday; 12:30–5:30 P.M., Sunday. *October–December:* 9:00 A.M.–6:00 P.M., Monday–Thursday; 9:00 A.M.–8:00 P.M., Friday; 8:00 A.M.–8:00 P.M., Saturday; 12:30–5:30 P.M., Sunday.
Outlets:
Banister Shoes
Black & Decker
Bon Worth
Corning Revere
Easy Spirit & Co.
Jewelry Outlet
Ocean Galleries
Paper Factory
Prestige Fragrance & Cosmetics, PFC Fragrance
Van Heusen
Vanity Fair, VF Factory Outlet
Credit Cards: MasterCard, Visa

Personal Checks: Yes, with proper identification (at the Vanity Fair outlet); check policies vary by store
Food: Fast food available in the area
Bus Tours: Member, National Tour Association, Inc.
Notes or Attractions: Within one hour of Panama City Beaches and direct route to I–10

Key Largo

Acme Boot Factory Outlet
102700 Overseas Highway 1

Directions: Take turnpike south until it ends at U.S. Highway 1. Continue south to mile marker 102. Outlet is on right.
Phone: (615) 552–2000, ext. 267
Hours: 9:00 A.M.–9:00 P.M., Monday–Sunday
Credit Cards: American Express, Discover, MasterCard, Visa
Personal Checks: Yes, with valid driver's license or other form of identification
Food: In vicinity
Bus Tours: Yes; advance notice appreciated
Notes or Attractions: State Park across the highway

Kissimmee

Aileen
Manufacturers Outlet Center
2557 Old Vineland Road

Directions: U.S. Highway 192, east of Route 535. Store located at Manufacturers Outlet Center.
Phone: (407) 396–2540
Hours: 9:30 A.M.–10:00 P.M., Monday–Saturday; 11:00 A.M.–5:00 P.M., Sunday
Credit Cards: MasterCard, Visa

Personal Checks: Yes
Food: Fast food in the immediate area
Bus Tours: Yes. Ask about a coupon book.
Notes or Attractions: Disney World, Universal Studios, Sea World—all nearby

Totes Factory Store
Kissimmee Manufacturers Mall
2503 Old Vineland Road

Directions: From I–4, take 192 Kissimmee exit, east, approximately 5 miles on the left. Look for bright yellow-and-green awning.
Phone: (407) 397–0530
Hours: *January–May* and *September–December:* 10:00 A.M.–9:00 P.M., Monday–Saturday; 11:00 A.M.–5:00 P.M., Sunday. *June–August:* 9:30 A.M.–10:00 P.M., Monday–Saturday.
Credit Cards: Discover, MasterCard, Visa
Personal Checks: Yes, with driver's license and major credit card
Food: In the immediate area
Bus Tours: Yes. A discount/coupon book from participating outlets is given to tour groups.
Notes or Attractions: Disney World fifteen minutes away; several dinner theaters and shows within 2 miles; Go-cart tracks nearby; twelve-screen movie theater nearby

Largo

Pixie Playmates
Plaza De Sunus

Directions: Route 275 to Highway 688, west to Belcher Road. Outlet is on the northeast corner of Highway 688 and Belcher.
Phone: (813) 531–1411
Hours: 10:00 A.M.–6:00 P.M., Monday–Saturday
Credit Cards: MasterCard, Visa
Personal Checks: Yes, if local

ATM: Yes, next door
Special Sales: $1.00 sales in the fall
Bus Tours: Yes
Notes or Attractions: Ten minutes away from Gulf of Mexico beaches

Naples

Coral Isle Factory Stores
State Route 951

Directions: 1 mile south of U.S. Highway 41 on State Route 951 to Marco Island
Phone: (813) 775–8083
Hours: 9:00 A.M.–8:00 P.M., Monday–Saturday; 10:00 A.M.–6:00 P.M., Sunday
Outlets:
Adolfo II
Aileen
Anne Klein
Bagmakers
Bass Shoes
Bon Worth
Boston Trader Kids
Cape Isle Knitters
Capezio
Chaus
Damon/Enro
Dansk
Etienne Aigner
Fieldcrest/Cannon
Geoffrey Beene
Gilligan & O'Malley
HE-RO Group
Islandgear
Jerzees

Jones New York
Kelly Stryker
L'eggs/Hanes/Bali
London Fog
Maidenform
Mikasa
Polly Flinders
Publisher's Warehouse
Rack Room Shoes
S & K Menswear
Tanner
Tie One On
Van Heusen
Villeroy & Boch
Westport
Whims
Credit Cards: Varies from store to store
Personal Checks: Varies from store to store
Food: Fast food
Bus Tours: Yes

North Palm Beach

Ribbon Outlet
Palm Beach Outlet Mall

Directions: From the turnpike, take Okeechobee exit, east on Okee-chobee Boulevard. Go one light; the outlet will be on the right.
Phone: (407) 684–5700
Hours: Call for information
Credit Cards: MasterCard, Visa
Personal Checks: Yes, with proper identification
Food: In the immediate area

Ocala

Acme Boot Factory Outlet
3890 NW Blitchton Road

Directions: Located on the west side of I–75 and the U.S. Highway 27 intersection. Outlet is ¼ mile on the left, next to Steinbrenner's Yankee Inn.
Phone: (615) 552–2000, ext. 267
Hours: 9:00 A.M.–9:00 P.M., Monday–Saturday; 9:00 A.M.–7:00 P.M., Sunday
Credit Cards: American Express, Discover, MasterCard, Visa
Personal Checks: Yes, with valid driver's license or other identification
Food: Nice restaurants and fast-food establishments in close proximity
Bus Tours: Yes, but park at the side of the building; truckers welcome
Notes or Attractions: Visitors are in the hub of Florida's horse country. Silver Springs Park is close by, with the largest freshwater springs in the United States. Glass-bottom boat rides available.

Orlando

Belz Factory Outlet Mall and Annex
5401 West Oakridge Road

Directions: From downtown Orlando, take I–4 west to the Kirkman Road exit; turn left onto Kirkman Road (435 South), then left onto International Drive; the mall is 1 mile ahead. From Disney World, take I–4 east to the International Drive exit; turn left onto International Drive; mall is 1 mile ahead. From airport, take Beeline Highway west to International Drive exit. Stay on International Drive to the north end. From Universal Studios, take right on Kirkman Road, then left on International Drive; mall is 1 mile ahead.
Phone: (407) 352–9611
Hours: 10:00 A.M.–9:00 P.M., Monday–Saturday; 10:00 A.M.–6:00 P.M., Sunday

Outlets:

Accessories
Accessorize
Anne Klein
Bag and Baggage
Etienne Aigner
Import-Export Exchange
Leather Loft
Swank
Totes
Wallet Works

Books, Records, and Tapes
Bookland Book Outlet
Book Warehouse
Music 4 Less

Cameras and Electronics
Electronics Outlet
Wolf Camera & Video

Family Wear (Men's, Women's, and Children's)
Adolfo II
Aileen
Barbizon Lingerie
Bon Worth
Boston Trader Kids
Bugle Boy
Burlington Brands
Calvin Klein
Cape Isle Knitters
Carole Hochman Lingerie
Carole Little
Carter's
Chaus
Children's Place
County Seat
CYA

Danskin
Dress Barn
Dress Barn Woman
Duck Head
Ducks Unlimited
Everything but Water
Fashion Mart
Geoffrey Beene
Guess?
harvé benard
Hit or Miss
Jerzees
Jockey
Jonathan Logan
Jordache
Just Kids
Kuppenheimer Men's Clothiers
L'eggs/Hanes/Bali
Leslie Fay
Levi's
London Fog
Maidenform
Menswear, Inc.
$9.99 Stockroom
No Nonsense & More
OshKosh B'Gosh (The Genuine Article)
Polly Flinders
S & K Menswear
SBX
Socks Galore
Today's Child
Van Heusen
Westport
Young Generations

Footwear
Bally

Banister Shoes
Bass Shoes
Capezio
Converse Shoe
Dexter Shoes
Frugal Frank's Shoe Outlet
General Shoe Factory to You
Reebok
Sneakee Feet
Unisa

Health and Beauty Aids
Anne Klein
Nutrition Outlet
Optical Outlet
Perfumania
Prestige Fragrance & Cosmetics,
    PFC Fragrance

Housewares
Brighter Side
Corning Revere
Farberware
Fieldcrest/Cannon
Fitz and Floyd
Kitchen Collection

Kitchen Place
Knife Factory
Mikasa
Oneida
Paper Factory
Pfaltzgraff
Tropic Art
Welcome Home

Jewelry
Crown Jewels
Diamonds Unlimited
Price Jewelers
Whims

Sportswear and Equipment
Bike Athletic
Sports Page

Toys/Gifts/Souvenirs
A & K Gift
Toy Liquidators

Variety
Everything's A Dollar

Due to corporate restrictions as outlined by this outlet mall, the publisher has been unable to provide profiles on the following outlets. These outlets have also been omitted from the indexes.

The Answer
Brown Shoe Co.
Bruno Magli
Buy Best
Carousel
Character Warehouse
Chicago Cutlery

Craig Sports
Electronics
Everthing Intimate
Factory Brand Shoe
Fragrance Outlet
Group USA
Henry Grethal

Historical Research
Jewelry Factory
Lee Winter
Liberty Marketing
Nature Made
Phil's Shoes
Rainbow Apparel
Rock and Mineral
San Francisco MB
Sbarro
Sergio Tacchini

Shoe World
Southern Key
Sunglass Express
Surf Jungle
Today's Woman
T-Shirt Factory
Vistana
Watch Works
Watches Plus
Westgate

Credit Cards: Most major credit cards
Personal Checks: Yes, with proper identification
Food: One sit down restaurant and numerous kiosks
Bus Tours: Yes
Notes or Attractions: Belz Factory Outlet Mall and Annex in Orlando is the state's second-largest tourist attraction, drawing approximately twelve million people per year. The 700,000-square-foot center, which includes two enclosed malls and four strip centers, is located at the north end of International Drive in Orlando's most popular tourist area. Area attractions include Disney World/Epcot, Universal Studios, Wet N Wild, and numerous hotels and restaurants.

Dansk Factory Outlet
7024 International Drive

Directions: From Orlando, take I–4 west to Route 435 exit (right). Take first right onto International Drive. Approximately three-quarters of a mile on right.
Phone: (407) 351–2425
Hours: 9:00 A.M.–7:00 P.M., Monday–Saturday; 11:00 A.M.–6:00 P.M., Sunday
Credit Cards: MasterCard, Visa
Personal Checks: Yes
Food: A large variety in the immediate area
Bus Tours: Yes
Notes and Attractions: Disney World fifteen minutes away, beaches within one hour

Jonathan Logan Outlet
4949 International Drive

Directions: Follow I–4 to International Drive
Phone: (407) 351–6687
Hours: 10:00 A.M.–9:00 P.M., Monday–Saturday; 10:00 A.M.–6:00 P.M., Sunday
Credit Cards: MasterCard, Visa
Personal Checks: Yes
Food: Immediately accessible
Bus Tours: Yes
Notes or Attractions: Many attractions, including Disney World

Lenox Factory Outlet
International Station
5247 International Drive

Directions: Off I–4, take exit 30A, Kirkman Road. Turn left on International Drive. Outlet is approximately half a mile on left.
Phone: (407) 354–5233
Hours: 9:00 A.M.–8:00 P.M., Monday–Saturday; 11:00 A.M.–6:00 P.M., Sunday
Credit Cards: Discover, MasterCard, Visa
Personal Checks: Yes
Food: Fast food nearby
Bus Tours: Yes
Notes or Attractions: Ten minutes from Disney World, five minutes from Universal Studios

Quality Outlet Center
International Drive

Directions: On International Drive, 1 block east of Kirkman Road (435). Traveling west on I–4, exit 435 south. Turn left at traffic light. Traveling east on I–4, exit International Drive. Turn left at traffic light.
Hours: 9:30 A.M.–9:00 P.M., Monday–Saturday; 11:00 A.M.–6:00 P.M., Sunday

Outlets:
American Tourister
Arrow Factory Store
Book Warehouse
Childcraft
Corning Revere
Florsheim Shoe
Great Western Boot
Laura Ashley
Le Creuset
Linens 'n Things
Magnavox
Manhattan
Mikasa
Perfumania
Royal Doulton
Sunglass World
Totes
Villeroy & Boch
Yes Brazil
Credit Cards: Varies by outlet
Personal Checks: Varies by outlet
Food: Fast food on-site
Bus Tours: Yes
Notes or Attractions: Closest factory outlet center to Universal Studios, International Drive hotels, Sea World, and Walt Disney World

Palm Harbor

Pixie Playmates
Palms Plaza

Directions: U.S. Highway 19 North. Outlet located at the northwest corner of Tampa Road, State Route 504.
Phone: (813) 531–1411
Hours: 10:00 A.M.–6:00 P.M., Monday–Saturday

Credit Cards: MasterCard, Visa
Personal Checks: Yes, if local
Special Sales: $1.00 sales in the fall
Bus Tours: Yes
Notes or Attractions: Near the Gulf of Mexico beaches

Panama City

Panama City Outlet Center
105 West Twenty-third Street

Directions: Located 1 mile west of Highway 231, near the Panama City Mall
Phone: Not available to public
Hours: *Summer:* 9:00 A.M.–9:00 P.M., Monday–Saturday; 11:00 A.M.–6:00 P.M., Sunday. *Winter:* 10:00 A.M.–9:00 P.M., Monday–Saturday; 11:00 A.M.–5:00 P.M., Sunday.
Outlets:
Aileen
Bass Shoes
Capezio
Corning Revere
Langtry
London Fog
Polly Flinders
Prestige Fragrance & Cosmetics, PFC Fragrance
Publisher's Warehouse
Russell Mills
Van Heusen
Credit Cards: American Express, Discover, MasterCard, Visa
Personal Checks: Yes
Food: In the immediate area
Bus Tours: Yes
Notes or Attractions: Panama City beaches and amusement parks nearby

Panama City Beach

Bealls
7038 W. Highway 98

Directions: From Highway 98 in Panama City, cross the Hathaway Bridge. Continue to Hathaway Crossing shopping complex on the right, just before you reach Thomas Drive. The outlet is located next to Kmart.
Phone: (904) 233–2924
Hours: 9:00 A.M.–9:00 P.M., Monday–Saturday; 12:00–5:00 P.M., Sunday
Credit Cards: Bealls, Discover, MasterCard, Visa
Personal Checks: Yes, with proper identification
Food: Fast food available in the immediate area
Bus Tours: Yes
Notes or Attractions: Within minutes of a variety of recreational opportunities and "The World's Most Beautiful Beaches" and St. Andrew Bay

St. Augustine

Acme Boot
2656 State Road 16

Directions: From I–95, take exit 95. Turn left. Outlet is ¼ mile off exit.
Phone: (615) 552–2000, ext. 267
Hours: 9:00 A.M.–9:00 P.M., Monday–Saturday; 10:00 A.M.–6:00 P.M., Sunday
Credit Cards: American Express, Discover, MasterCard, Visa
Personal Checks: Yes, with valid driver's license or other identification
Food: Restaurants and fast-food establishments in the immediate area
Bus Tours: Yes
Notes or Attractions: Enjoy the historic district of this area.

Aileen

St. Augustine Outlet Center
2700 State Road 16, Suite 5

Directions: From I–95, take exit 95. Follow signs to outlet center, approximately 1 mile.
Phone: (904) 829–9248
Hours: 9:00 A.M.–9:00 P.M., Monday–Saturday; 10:00 A.M.–6:00 P.M., Sunday
Credit Cards: MasterCard, Visa
Personal Checks: Yes
Food: Yes, a food court is in the center.
Bus Tours: Yes. Ask about a coupon book.
Notes or Attractions: Beach is twenty minutes away. Historical downtown St. Augustine is 10 miles away.

Arrow Factory Store

St. Augustine Outlet Center
2700 State Road 16, Space 705

Directions: From I–95, take exit 95. Follow signs to outlet center, approximately 1 mile.
Phone: (940) 824–0910
Hours: 9:00 A.M.–9:00 P.M., Monday–Saturday; 10:00 A.M.–6:00 P.M., Sunday
Credit Cards: MasterCard, Visa
Personal Checks: Yes
Food: Yes, at food court
Bus Tours: Yes

South Daytona

Aileen
South Daytona Beach Outlet Mall
2400 S. Ridgewood Avenue, S-38

Directions: Off I–95, take exit 87 onto Highway 400. Go south about 1 mile to Daytona Beach Outlet Mall.
Phone: (904) 756–3055
Hours: 10:00 A.M.–9:00 P.M., Monday–Saturday; 12:00–6:00 P.M., Sunday
Credit Cards: MasterCard, Visa
Personal Checks: Yes
Food: Yes, food court available
Bus Tours: Yes. Ask about a coupon book.
Notes or Attractions: Disney World, one hour away; beach, ten minutes away; dog track, fifteen minutes away; jai alai, fifteen minutes away.

Sunrise

Sawgrass Mills Outlet Mall
12801 West Sunrise Boulevard

Directions: Located only 9 miles west of Ft. Lauderdale; convenient access from Miami and West Palm Beach. Take I–95 to Sunrise Boulevard and go west 9 miles.
Phone: (305) 846–2300 or (800) FL–MILLS
Hours: 10:00 A.M.–9:30 P.M., Monday–Saturday; 11:00 A.M.–6:00 P.M., Sunday
Outlets: Sawgrass Mills is the world's largest outlet mall, with more than 200 stores within 2.2 million square feet. All stores offer discounts of 20 to 70 percent. Spiegel's Outlet Store, Macy's Close-Out, Sak's Clearing House, Marshalls, Waccamaw, Brandsmart USA, Phar-Mor, Vanity Fair Factory Outlet, Sears Outlet, and more!

Aileen
American Tourister
Athlete's Foot
Bag and Baggage
Banister Shoes
Barbizon Lingerie
Book Warehouse
Brass Factory
Bugle Boy
Carter's
County Seat
CYA
Dexter Shoes
Dress Barn
Dress Barn Woman
Eddie Bauer
Etienne Aigner
Everything's A Dollar I
Everything's A Dollar II
Famous Footwear
Guess?
Helen's Handbags
I.B. Diffusion

Jewelry Outlet
J. G. Hook
Joan & David
Levi's
Maidenform
$9.99 Stockroom
9 West
No Nonsense & More
Publisher's Book Outlet/
    Card Barn
Rack Room Shoes
Sneakee Feet
Starbaby
Sun Shades 501, Ltd.
Top of the Line Fragrances and
    Cosmetics
Toy Liquidators
Van Heusen
Vanity Fair
Welcome Home
Westport
Whims

Due to corporate restrictions as outlined by this outlet mall, the publisher has been unable to provide profiles on the following outlets. These outlets also have been deleted from the indexes.

Aca Joe
Accessory Warehouse
American Newsstand
Ann Taylor Clearance Center
The Answer
Art Depot
Art Works
Athletic Footwear
Ball Park Productions
Baron's Outlet

Beall's Outlet
Bed Bath & Beyond
Bedlington Investments, Ltd.
Bentley's Luggage Outlet
Best Wishes
Biblio-Tee
Bostonian Hanover Shoe
Burt's Jewelers
Cathay House
Chain Reaction Jewelers

Chico's Outlet
Cirage
Claire's Boutique
Clandestine of Argentina
Class Perfumes
Clothestime
Club Shop
Cohen's Fashion Optical
Collector's Showroom
Cuban Supreme
Cypress Factory Outlet
Designer's Row Unlimited
Discount Luggage Outlet
Eagles Fashion Club
Electronics Boutique
Eye of the Hurricane
Fadz
Famous Brands
Fan Club
Fayva Shoes
5-7-9 Outlet
Flag Shop
Flamingo Gallery
Fragrance Outlet
The Garage
Glamour Shots
GNC (General Nutrition Center)
Gotcha Good
Half Time
Importers Area Rug Outlet
J.B.'s Boutique
Jewelmasters Department Store
Kay-Bee Toys
Kids Mart Clearance Center
Leather Shop
Lillie Rubin
Luria's Jewelry Exchange
MCO (Macy's Close-Out)

Maraolo
Merry-Go-Round
Miami Shoes
Mr. Bulky
National Jewelry Sales
No? Yes!
Obenna
One Stop Fashions
OptiDesign
Originals by Reina
Palm Club
Pampered Lady
Panda Express
Payless Shoe Source
Pewter Place
Phil's Shoes
Pro Image
Remington
Ritz Camera
Rori
Salz on the Avenue
Scribbles Outlet
Secaucus Handbags
Security Works
Segrets Outlet
Sergio's Gallery
Sher-Al's Boutique
Small Delights
Small Wonders
S.M. T-Shirt Factory
Sock Kingdom
Specs Music & Movies
Sports Authority
Sportswear Unlimited
Square Circle
Sun Day Best
Swim 'n Sport Outlet
Tahari

Tee Pee Western Wear
Today's Woman
Touchdown Jewelers
Toy Works
Trend Club
Trends
Venez Shoe Outlet
Vitamin World
Westport Woman
Wet Seal
Credit Cards: All accepted
Personal Checks: Yes, with identification
Food: Two large food courts, plus three full-service restaurants
Bus Tours: Yes, meal and gift certificates for drivers and escorts, plus coupon book and shopping bag for everyone on the bus
Notes or Attractions: Near the Everglades and Ft. Lauderdale. On the property is an eighteen-cinema Cobb movie theater, plus Everglades Holiday Park, Flamingo Gardens, Butterfly World, and Ft. Lauderdale beaches.

Tampa

Acme Boot Factory Outlet
3613 Busch Boulevard

Directions: Right across from Busch Gardens
Phone: (615) 552-2000, ext. 267
Hours: 10:00 A.M.–9:00 P.M., Monday–Saturday; 11:00 A.M.–6:00 P.M., Sunday
Credit Cards: American Express, Discover, MasterCard, Visa
Personal Checks: Yes, with valid driver's license or other form of identification
Food: In vicinity
Bus Tours: Yes; advance notice appreciated
Notes or Attractions: Busch Gardens is an exciting tourist attraction across the street.

Acme Boot Factory Outlet
3219 North Monroe Street

Directions: From I–10, take exit 29, U.S. Highway 27 North. Outlet is three-quarters of a mile on right. Sam's Wholesale Club is next door.
Phone: (615) 552–2000, ext. 267
Hours: 9:00 A.M.–9:00 P.M., Monday–Saturday; 10:00 A.M.–6:00 P.M., Sunday
Credit Cards: American Express, Discover, MasterCard, Visa
Personal Checks: Yes, with a valid driver's license or other identification
Food: Restaurants and fast-food establishments in the immediate area
Bus Tours: Yes

University Park

Aileen
Sarasota Outlet Center
8231 Cooper Creek Boulevard

Directions: From I–75, take exit 40. The outlet is approximately a quarter-mile west.
Phone: (813) 355–9190
Hours: 10:00 A.M.–9:00 P.M., Monday–Saturday; 12:00–6:00 P.M., Sunday
Credit Cards: MasterCard, Visa
Personal Checks: Yes
Food: Yes, food court on the premises
Bus Tours: Yes. Ask about a coupon book.
Notes or Attractions: Beaches thirty minutes away; dog races nearby; John Ringley Museum in immediate area

Dansk
8471 Cooper Creek Boulevard

Directions: From I–75, take exit 40, University Parkway
Phone: (813) 359–2284

Hours: 10:00 A.M.–9:00 P.M., Monday–Saturday; 12:00–6:00 P.M., Sunday
Credit Cards: MasterCard, Visa
Personal Checks: Yes
Food: Yes, food court on premises
Bus Tours: Yes. Parking provided with driver's lounge.
Note or Attractions: Five minutes from Sarasota/Bradenton International Airport, fifteen minutes from beaches

Lenox

Sarasota Outlet Center

Directions: From I–75, take exit 40 (University Parkway). First street on the right.
Phone: (813) 359–8655
Hours: 10:00 A.M.–9:00 P.M., Monday–Saturday
Credit Cards: Discover, MasterCard, Visa
Personal Checks: Yes, with driver's license and expiration date on a current credit card
ATM: Nearby
Food: Yes, food court on premises
Bus Tours: Yes. Contact mall office (813) 359–2050.
Notes or Attractions: Located in Sarasota, the cultural center of the Florida west coast; near beaches

Ribbon Outlet

Sarasota Outlet Center

Directions: From I–75, take exit 40. Outlet is about a quarter-mile west.
Phone: (813) 359–8303
Hours: 10:00 A.M.–9:00 P.M., Monday–Saturday
Credit Cards: MasterCard, Visa
Personal Checks: Yes, with proper identification
Food: Yes, in the immediate area
Bus Tours: Yes, at the center

West Palm Beach

Aileen
Palm Beach Outlet Center
5700 Okeechobee Boulevard

Directions: Follow Florida Turnpike to exit 99. Turn left at the first traffic light. Outlet center will be on your left, less than a mile.
Phone: (407) 687–4434
Hours: 10:00 A.M.–7:00 P.M., Monday–Saturday; 12:00–5:00 P.M., Sunday
Credit Cards: MasterCard, Visa
Personal Checks: Yes
Food: Yes, food court on premises
Bus Tours: Yes. Ask about a coupon book.
Notes or Attractions: Lion Country Safari 5 miles away

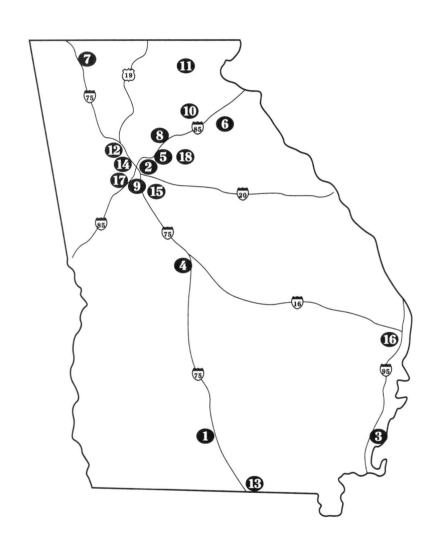

Georgia

Numbers at the left of this legend correspond to the numbers on the accompanying map. The number to the right of each city's or town's name is the page number on which that municipality's outlets first appear in this book.

1. Adel, 106
2. Atlanta, 107
3. Brunswick, 108
4. Byron, 109
5. Chamblee, 110
6. Commerce, 111
7. Dalton, 113
8. Duluth, 120
9. Forest Park, 121

10. Gainesville, 121
11. Helen, 122
12. Kennesaw, 123
13. Lake Park, 124
14. Marietta, 126
15. Morrow, 127
16. Savannah, 127
17. Smyrna, 128
18. Stone Mountain, 129

For Your Information

The Public Relations Coordinator of the Georgia Department of Industry, Trade and Tourism provides a very helpful *Georgia Factory and Discount Outlet Guide*. Only names and addresses are provided, with no phone numbers, zip codes, or directions—but it is geographically segmented across the state. The listing includes not only factory outlets, but "off-price" outlets as well as entries for food and farmer's market–type information.

There is a disclaimer on the guide that reads: "Considerable effort has been made to compile and verify a complete list of Georgia's Outlet and Discount Stores. The Georgia Department of Industry, Trade and Tourism does not accept responsibility for credibility of individual stores."

To receive a copy of this booklet, write to Georgia Department of Industry, Trade and Tourism, Post Office Box 177, Atlanta, GA 30301–1776; or phone (404) 656–3590.

Adel

Factory Stores Adel
I–75 at exit 10

Directions: Going north on I–75, take exit 10 at Highway 37.
Phone: (912) 896–4848
Hours: 8:00 A.M.–9:00 P.M., Monday–Sunday
Outlets:
Aileen
Arrow Factory Store
Bon Worth
Book Sale
Boots 'n Brims
Christmas Factory
Diamond Jim's Jewelry
Hush Puppies
Izod

Judy Bond Blouses
King Frog
M.C. Sox
Credit Cards: MasterCard, Visa
Personal Checks: Yes, with proper identification
Food: Yes, restaurants and fast food in the immediate area
Bus Tours: Yes, with banquet and meeting facilities available; special bus parking at the Days Inn
Notes or Attractions: Located in southern Georgia on the Florida border

Atlanta

Barry Manufacturing Company
4505 Fulton Industrial Boulevard

Directions: I–20 to Fulton Industrial Boulevard. One mile on the right.
Phone: (404) 696–1680
Hours: 9:00 A.M.–6:00 P.M., Monday–Saturday; 12:00–5:00 P.M., Sunday
Credit Cards: American Express, Discover, MasterCard, Visa
Personal Checks: Yes
Food: Nearby
Bus Tours: Yes
Notes or Attractions: Atlanta offers something for everyone in the way of excitement and activity.

Ribbon Outlet
Gwinnett Marketfair

Directions: From I–85 north, take exit at Pleasant Hill Road. Turn left and travel approximately ½ mile. Outlet is on the left.
Phone: (404) 233–1902
Hours: Call for information.
Credit Cards: MasterCard, Visa
Personal Checks: Yes, with proper identification
Food: Yes, in the immediate area

Brunswick

Outlets Ltd. Mall
I–95, exit 7A

Directions: Located off I–95, at the intersection of exit 7A and Highway 341
Phone: (912) 264–6842
Hours: 9:00 A.M.–9:00 P.M., Monday–Saturday; 1:00–6:00 P.M., Sunday
Outlets:
Aileen
American Tourister
Bass Shoes
Black & Decker
Bon Worth
Book Warehouse
Bugle Boy
Chaus
Corning Revere
Duck Head
Famous Footwear
Leather Loft
L'eggs/Hanes/Bali
Leslie Fay
Manhattan
Prestige Fragrance & Cosmetics, PFC Fragrance
Rack Room Shoes
Ribbon Outlet
S & K Menswear
Stone Mountain Handbag
Tie One On
Van Heusen
Welcome Home
Westport
Credit Cards: Varies from store to store
Personal Checks: Varies from store to store
Food: Yes, fast food
Bus Tours: Yes

Notes or Attractions: This location is close to beaches and to Jekyll and St. Simons islands.

Byron

Peach Festival Outlet Center
311 Highway 49N

Directions: Located 12 miles south of Macon, at Highway 49 (exit 46) and I–75
Phone: (912) 956–1855
Hours: 9:00 A.M.–9:00 P.M., Monday–Saturday; 11:00 A.M –6:00 P.M., Sunday
Outlets:
Aileen
American Tourister
Banister Shoes
Barbizon Lingerie
Bass Shoes
Bon Worth
Book Warehouse
Bugle Boy
Champion-Hanes
Corning Revere
Dress Barn
Dress Barn Woman
Duck Head
Fashion Direct
Fieldcrest/Cannon
Jonathan Logan
Kids Biz
Kitchen Collection
L'eggs/Hanes/Bali
Levi's
Little Red Shoe House (Wolverine)
Paper Factory

Prestige Fragrance & Cosmetics, PFC Fragrance
Rack Room Shoes
Ribbon Outlet
S & K Menswear
Toy Liquidators
Van Heusen
Welcome Home
Credit Cards: MasterCard, Visa
Personal Checks: Normally yes, with a major credit card
ATMs: Yes for Cirrus
Food: Yogurt and fast food in the center
Bus Tours: Yes; bus drivers eat free at Yogurt House and Byron Plantation Store.
Notes or Attractions: Warner Air Force Base; an emphasis on the peach industry in the area; and Massee Lane Gardens in nearby Ft. Valley.

Chamblee

Barry Manufacturing Company
2303 John Glenn Drive

Directions: Off Peachtree Industrial Boulevard, ¾ mile inside I–285 on John Glenn Drive
Phone: (404) 457–8992
Hours: 9:00 A.M.–6:00 P.M., Monday–Saturday (until 9:00 Thursday); 12:00–5:00 P.M., Sunday
Credit Cards: American Express, Discover, MasterCard, Visa
Personal Checks: Yes
Food: Fast food nearby
Bus Tours: Yes
Notes or Attractions: Minutes from the shopping and excitement of downtown Atlanta

Commerce

Commerce Factory Stores
Highway 441

Directions: I–85, exit 53 onto Highway 441
Outlets:
Arrow Factory Store
Book Warehouse
Carter's
Coats and Clark
Dan River
Dansk
Duck Head
Florsheim Shoe
Fruit of the Loom
Gold Toe
Izod
Jonathan Logan
Kitchen Collections
Lenox
Magnavox
NCS Shoe
Olga/Warner's
Polly Flinders
Prestige Fragrance & Cosmetics, PFC Fragrance
S & K Menswear
Victoria Creations
Westport
Credit Cards: Varies by store
Personal Checks: Varies by store
Food: Yes, in the immediate area
Bus Tours: Yes
Notes or Attractions: Within an hour's drive of Atlanta; halfway between Atlanta and Greenville, South Carolina

Tanger Factory Outlet Center
I–85, exit 53

Directions: Take I–85 to exit 53; look for the red roofs just off the exit.
Phone: (404) 335–4537
Hours: 9:00 A.M.–9:00 P.M., Monday–Saturday; 12:00–6:00 P.M., Sunday
Outlets:
Adolfo II
Aileen
American Tourister
Banister Shoes
Barbizon Lingerie
Bass Shoes
Black & Decker
Bruce Alan Bags
Bugle Boy
Cape Isle Knitters
Champion-Hanes
Chaus
Corning Revere
Farberware, Inc.
Fieldcrest/Cannon
Geoffrey Beene
harvé benard
Jerzees
Just Kids
L'eggs/Hanes/Bali
Leslie Fay
Levi's
Liz Claiborne
London Fog
Maidenform
Manhattan
Mikasa
Multiples
Oneida
OshKosh B'Gosh (The Genuine Article)
Paper Factory

Reebok
Ribbon Outlet
Socks Galore and More
Top of the Line Fragrances and Cosmetics
Toy Liquidators
Van Heusen
Wallet Works
Welcome Home
Credit Cards: American Express, MasterCard, and Visa accepted by most of the stores
Personal Checks: Yes, with driver's license and major credit cards as identification
Food: Restaurant adjacent to property
Bus Tours: Yes, very welcome. Incentive program for tour guide and bus driver. Free meal for tour guide and bus driver if tour group eats at Shoney's.
Notes or Attractions: Free parking; mall-walkers program; customer lounge; monthly special promotions.

Dalton

Dalton Factory Stores
Interstate 75

Directions: Take exit 136. Outlet is located at I–75 and Walnut Avenue.
Phone: (706) 278–0399
Hours: *January–February:* 9:00 A.M.–7:00 P.M., Monday–Thursday; 9:00 A.M.–9:00 P.M., Friday–Saturday; 12:00–6:00 P.M., Sunday. *March–December:* 9:00 A.M.–9:00 P.M., Monday–Saturday; 12:00–6:00 P.M., Sunday.
Outlets:
Accessory Stop
Aileen
American Tourister
Banister Shoes
Barbizon Lingerie
Bass Shoes

Book Warehouse
Boot Factory
Bugle Boy
Cape Isle Knitters
Champion-Hanes
Corning Revere
Duck Head
Farberware, Inc.
Florsheim Shoe
Greetings 'N' More
Izod
Jonathan Logan
Jones New York
Kelly Stryker
L'eggs/Hanes/Bali
Prestige Fragrance & Cosmetics, PFC Fragrance
Rack Room Shoes
Ribbon Outlet
S & K Menswear
Toy Liquidators
Van Heusen
Welcome Home
West Point Pepperell Bed, Bath and Linens Factory Outlet
Westport
Young Generations

Credit Cards: Varies by store, but most accept American Express, Discover, MasterCard, and Visa

Personal Checks: Yes, with proper identification

Food: Yes

Bus Tours: Eighteen nationally known restaurants; five hotels and five service stations at this exit

Note: Dalton is known as the "Carpet Capital of the World." The types of carpets manufactured in Dalton are diverse. There are tufted carpets, bedroom carpets, commercial carpets, patterned carpets, chenille spreads, Oriental rugs, and floor coverings and finishings. The city has more than 200 manufacturing plants and more than 100 outlets. To receive complete information on outlet shopping in Dalton, contact the Dalton Convention and Visitors Bureau, P.O. Box 2046, 2211 Dug Gap

Battle Road, Dalton, Georgia 30722; (706) 272–7676. Savings of up to 60 percent can be expected.

The following are chamber of commerce members of the Carpet Outlets of Dalton. The *s highlight those who are also members of the Carpet & Rug Outlet Council, a program of the Dalton-Whitfield Chamber of Commerce.

* A & W Carpet Sales & Service
David Dunn
550 Conway Street
Dalton, GA 30720
(404) 278–7660

* Access Carpets
David Jamison
3068 N. Dug Gap Road
Dalton, GA 30722
(706) 277–3352
(800) 433–8479

Ashley's Carpet Direct
James M. Brown
3006 Parquet Road, exit 135
Dalton, GA 30720
(706) 277–5590
(800) 451–8756
Fax: (706) 226–8592

Baker's Carpet Gallery
Terry Baker
693 Varnell Road
Tunnel Hill, GA 30755
(706) 673–2343

* Bearden Bros. Carpet & Textile Corporation
Rod Bearden
3200-A Dug Gap Road, Southwest
#A, exit 135
Dalton, GA 30722
(706) 277–3265
(800) 433–0074

Beaver Carpets
Dennis Garrison
695 Varnell Road
Tunnel Hill, GA 30755
(706) 673–2366
(800) 633–5238

* Beckler's Carpet Outlet
Randy Beckler
3051 N. Dug Gap Road, exit 135
Dalton, GA 30722
(706) 277–1151
(800) BECKLER

Black's Carpet, Inc.
Steve Black
250 Connector 3
P.O. Box 1856
Dalton, GA 30722–1856
(706) 277–2505

* Blue Circle/Carpetown, Inc.
Ralph Whaley
1706 U.S. Highway 41 South
Dalton, GA 30720
(706) 226–7561
(800) 622–7561

* Britton Carpet Alley
Clyde Britton
3198 N. Dug Gap Road, exit 135
Dalton, GA 30722
(706) 277–3913
(800) 232–3913

Broadacre Carpet and Orientals
Don Hayes
703 N. Varnell Road, exit 138
Tunnel Hills, GA 30755
(706) 673–6588

* Brown's Carpets, Inc.
Earl Brown
2514 E. Walnut Avenue, exit 136
Dalton, GA 30722
(706) 278–5411

Bud's Carpets
Bud Rogers
3516 S. Dixie Highway
P.O. Box 1042
Dalton, GA 30722–1042
(702) 277–2676

* By-Pass Carpet
Jess Staton
3518 S. Dixie Highway
Dalton, GA 30722
(706) 277–3336
(800) 772–1894

* C & L Industries/Access Carpets
David L. Jamison
3068 N. Dug Gap Road
P.O. Box 481
Dalton, GA 30722–0481
(706) 277–3352
(800) 433–8479

Carpet America
Ron Stansell
114 N. Adella Drive
P.O. Box 4268
Dalton, GA 30719–4268
(706) 278–1116
(800) 554–4574

* Carpet Discount Center, Inc.
Don Anderson
3035 Old Dug Gap Road, exit 135
Dalton, GA 30722
(706) 277–1279
(800) 347–0683

* Carpet Express
Murray Bandy
915 Market Street
Dalton, GA 30720
(706) 278–8507
(800) 922–5582

* Carpets American Made
Betty Black
3056 N. Dug Gap Road, exit 135
Dalton, GA 30722
(706) 277–2896
(800) 446–4096

* **Carpets by Sarah Ruth**
John Crump
2804-A E. Walnut Avenue
Dalton, GA 30722
(706) 226–2814
(800) 847–3476

* **Carpets of Dalton, Inc.**
Lamar Hennon
3010 Old Dug Gap Road, exit 135
Dalton, GA 30722
(706) 277–3132
(800) 262–3132

* **Carpet Wholesale Outlet**
Leland McClain
739 Varnell Road
Dalton, GA 30722
(706) 673–2112
(800) 628–4412

* **CISU of Dalton, Inc.**
Ed Johnson
3005 Parquel Road
P.O. Box 1068
Dalton, GA 30722–1068
(706) 277–1449
(800) 227–2478

Crown Carpet
Howard Padgett
Highway 76 East
Chatsworth, GA 30705
(706) 695–1440

Dalton Carpet Master
Dwight Patterson
3060 N. Dug Gap Road
Dalton, GA 30722
(706) 277–2700

Dalton GA Wholesale Carpets
Tim Norvell
3041 N. Dug Gap Rd., SW
Dalton, GA 30720
(706) 277–9559
(800) 476–9559

Dalyn Oriental Rugs
Bill and Judy Adams
2942 N. Dug Gap Road
Dalton, GA 30722
(706) 277–2909

Dennard Bros./Carpet Barn
Robert Dennard
3054 N. Dug Gap Road, exit 135
Dalton, GA 30722
(706) 277–3660
(800) 345–0478

Direct Dalton Carpets, Inc.
Bob Bailey
3425 Dug Gap Road
P.O. Box 2645
Dalton, GA 30722–2645
(706) 277–1200

Domestic & Export Carpet, Inc.
Jerry Nealey
2516 S. Dixie Highway
P.O. Box 1966
Dalton, GA 30722–1966
(706) 277–2672

The Floor Group, Inc.
Ronnie Booher
418 W. Hawthorne Street
Dalton, GA 30722
(706) 278–7299
(800) 322–7299

* Floor Trends
Rick King
919 S. Thornton Avenue, exit 136
Dalton, GA 30720
(706) 226–3444
(800) 462–6210

Hank's Carpet
Hank Pitts
691 Varnell Road, exit 138
Tunnel Hill, GA 30755
(706) 673–2410

* I–75 Carpets, Inc.
Bob Dailey/Ron Houston
3002 N. Dug Gap Road, exit 135
Dalton, GA 30720
(706) 277–2149
(800) 233–6286

Johnson's Carpets, Inc.
Roy G. Johnson
3239 S. Dixie Highway
Dalton, GA 30702
(706) 277–2775

*** Kinnaird & Francke Wholesale
   Carpets, Inc.**
Jerry Stanley
3021 S. Dug Gap Road, exit 135
Dalton, GA 30720
(706) 277–2599
(800) 423–1823

* Liberty Carpet Co., Inc.
Stephen and Shirley Herzfeld
3514 S. Dixie Highway
P.O. Box 1382
Dalton, GA 30722
(706) 277–9700
(800) 888–1249

Long's Carpet & Rug
Gene Long
2625 S. Dixie Highway, exit 135
Dalton, GA 30720
(706) 277–2552
(800) 545–5664

* Major Carpets, Inc.
John and Jean O'Neal
3018 N. Dug Gap Road, exit 135
Dalton, GA 30722
(706) 277–3341

* Michael's Carpets of Dalton
Jim Meadows
699 Varnell Road, exit 138
Tunnel Hill, GA 30755
(706) 673–6505
(800) 634–9509

* Myers Carpet Co., Inc.
Rick Myers
3096 N. Dug Gap Road, exit 135
Dalton, GA 30722
(706) 278–4053

Northwest Carpet, Inc.
Randall Coker
2001 James Court, NE
P.O. Box 1844
Dalton, GA 30722–1844
(706) 259–9486

Oriental Rug House
Nancy Strain
2173 Tunnel Hill–Varnell Road
Tunnel Hill, GA 30755
(706) 673–4224

Oriental Weavers
Mohamed Farid
3293 Lower Dug Gap Road
Dalton, GA 30720
(706) 277–9666

Owen Carpet Company
Gary Swanson
2752 Dug Gap Road, exit 135
Dalton, GA 30720
(706) 277–1321
(800) 626–6936

Paradise Mills, Inc.
David Burt
2601 Chattanooga Road, exit 137
Dalton, GA 30722–2488
(706) 226–9064
(800) 338–7811

Parker's Carpet, Inc.
Clifford Parker, Jr.
3200 Dug Gap Road, exit 135
Dalton, GA 30722
(706) 277–3091

* Peanut's Carpet House
D. H. Howard
3558 E. Walnut Avenue, exit 136
Dalton, GA 30721
(706) 278–8120

* Quality Discount Carpet
Ivan Carson, Jr./Betty Carson
1207 W. Walnut Avenue, exit 136
Dalton, GA 30722
(706) 226–7611
(800) 233–0993

S & S Mills
Danny Simmons
2650 Lakeland Road
P.O. Box 1568
Dalton, GA 30722–1568

SD Carpets/AJS Outdoor Advertising
Jimmy Doyle
1491 Mill Creek Road
Rocky Face, GA 30740
(706) 277–7980

Shaw Industries/Carpet Values Mill Outlet
Steve Roan
800 Abutment Road
Dalton, GA 30722
(706) 275–1334

* Southern Comfort Carpets
Denny Smith
1203 Broadrick Drive, Suite 210
Dalton, GA 30720
(706) 226–8359
(800) 749–5013

Tailor Made Carpets
Edna Young
1526 W. Walnut Avenue, exit 136
Dalton, GA 30722
(706) 226–4411

* Warehouse Carpets, Inc.
Ronnie Reece
2225 E. Walnut Avenue, exit 136
Dalton, GA 30721
(706) 226–2229
(800) 526–2229

* Whaley Carpet Outlet
Eddie & Vickie Whaley
109 Bryant Avenue, exit 136
Dalton, GA 30722
(706) 226–2730
(800) 422–2730

Duluth

I–85 Outlets Ltd. Mall
Pleasant Hill Road

Directions: Take exit 40 off I–85; the mall is nine minutes north of Atlanta, one block west of I–85 at Pleasant Hill and Venture Drive.
Phone: (404) 476–8552
Hours: 10:00 A.M.–9:00 P.M., Monday–Friday; 10:00 A.M.–6:00 P.M., Saturday; 12:00–6:00 P.M., Sunday
Outlets:
Burlington Coat Factory
Dress Barn
Guven Fine Jewelry
K & S Men's Liquidation
Old Mill
Sportswear Depot
Credit Cards: Varies by store
Personal Checks: Each outlet has its own policy
Food: Fast food available
Bus Tours: Yes
Notes or Attractions: Close to all Atlanta tourist sights; Big Hit (batting cage); next to the largest retail mall in the southeastern United States

Forest Park

JC Penney Catalog Outlet
5500 South Expressway

Directions: Take I–75 to exit 78 (Forest Parkway); take Frontage Road to the outlet (located south of the Farmers Market).
Phone: (404) 363–3855
Hours: 10:00 A.M.–9:00 P.M., Monday–Friday; 9:00 A.M.–9:00 P.M., Saturday; 12:00–6:00 P.M., Sunday
Credit Cards: American Express, Discover, JC Penney, MasterCard, Visa
Personal Checks: Yes
Food: No
Bus Tours: Yes; ample parking available
Notes or Attractions: Located five minutes south of the State Farmer's Market

Gainesville

Barry Manufacturing Company
2121 Brownsbridge Road

Directions: From downtown Gainesville, go south on Highway 13 to Highway 369, which is Brownsbridge Road.
Phone: (404) 534–7685
Hours: 9:00 A.M.–6:00 P.M., Monday–Saturday
Credit Cards: American Express, Discover, MasterCard, Visa
Personal Checks: Yes
Food: Fast food nearby
Bus Tours: Yes

Helen

Alpine Village Outlets
Highway 75, Main Street

Directions: From Gainesville, take Highway 129 north to Cleveland, then Highway 75 to Helen. From Georgia Highway 400, take Highway 115 to Cleveland, then Highway 75 to Helen.
Phone: Helen Chamber of Commerce, (404) 878–2181; management office, (404) 878–3016
Hours: *January–March:* 10:00 A.M.–6:00 P.M., Monday–Thursday; 10:00 A.M.–9:00 P.M., Friday–Saturday; 12:00–6:00 P.M., Sunday. *April–December:* 10:00 A.M.–9:00 P.M., Monday–Saturday; 12:00–6:00 P.M., Sunday.
Outlets:
Aileen
Alpine Festival of Arts & Crafts
Arrow Factory Store
Banister Shoes
Bass Shoes
Cape Isle Knitters
Carousel Books
Champion-Hanes
Corning Revere
Duck Head
Fashion Flair
Fieldcrest/Cannon
Gold & Gem Outlet
Habersham Vintners and Winery
Izod
Kitchen Collection
L'eggs/Hanes/Bali
Little Red Shoe House (Wolverine)
London Fog
Orbit
Prestige Fragrance & Cosmetics, PFC Fragrance
Puddle Jumpers
Ropers Clothing
Totes/Sunglass World

Toy Liquidators
Van Heusen
Westport
Credit Cards: MasterCard, Visa (some stores take Discover)
Personal Checks: Normally yes, with major credit cards
ATM: Local banks half a block from mall
Food: Yogurt and hot dogs within the mall; restaurants within walking distance
Alternate Transportation: Mall has free parking, and a privately owned trolley picks up and transports to the town shops.
Bus Tours: Yes. Bus drivers eat free at Yogurt Haus; discount coupons are available at the chamber of commerce.
Notes or Attractions: Within a half-hour's drive, enjoy hiking, fishing, golf, miniature golf, tubing on the river, and horseback riding. Pan for gold or visit Babyland General, home of the Cabbage Patch Kids. For seasonal activities, Octoberfest starts in September and ends in October; Fasching is a four-week festival in January; and Mayfest is held in May. Golf course five minutes away. State park 3 miles north. Scenic highway 3 miles north.

Kennesaw

Townfair Value Shops
3333 George Busbee Parkway

Directions: Take I–75 north from Atlanta to exit 117, then take a right at the end of the ramp and another right at the first traffic light on Chastain Road. Outlet mall is on the right.
Phone: (404) 424–9500
Hours: 10:00 A.M.–9:00 P.M., Monday–Saturday; 1:00–6:00 P.M., Sunday
Outlets:
Dress Barn
Famous Footwear
Finish Line
General Bookstore
Georgia Wholesale Furniture

Guven Fine Jewelry
Oak Towne Furniture
Paper Factory
Picture Framer
Van Heusen
Credit Cards: Acceptability varies by merchant
Personal Checks: Yes, but requirements vary by merchant
Food: Fast food
Bus Tours: Yes, parking available
Notes or Attractions: Near all the activity of Atlanta, Georgia; Mall Walkers Club; more stores to open in February 1994

Lake Park

Acme Boot Factory Outlet
1323 Lakes Boulevard

Directions: Follow I–75 south to Lake Park, exit 2 going north. Outlet is on the right.
Phone: (615) 552–2000, ext. 267
Hours: 9:00 A.M.–8:00 P.M., Monday–Saturday; 10:00 A.M.–6:00 P.M., Sunday
Credit Cards: American Express, Discover, MasterCard, Visa
Personal Checks: Yes, with valid driver's license or other identification
Food: Fast food, Chinese, pizza, and family-style food
Bus Tours: Yes
Notes or Attractions: Near Valdosta State College; twenty minutes from the Florida state line

Lake Park Mill Store Plaza
I–75, exit 2

Directions: Take I–75 to exit 2 in Lake Park; 18 miles south of Valdosta and 4 miles north of Georgia/Florida line.
Phone: (912) 559–6822

Hours: 9:00 A.M.–7:00 P.M., Monday–Saturday; 10:00 A.M.–6:00 P.M., Sunday

Outlets:
Aileen
American Tourister
Bass Shoes
Black & Decker
Bon Worth
Carter's
Converse Shoe
Corning Revere
Dansk
Dexter Shoes
Evan-Picone
Famous Brands Housewares
Famous Footwear
Fostoria
Full Size Fashions
Gold and Diamonds Direct
harvé benard
Henson Lingerie
Izod
Johnston & Murphy
Jonathan Logan
Kitchen Collection
Kuppenheimer Men's Clothiers
Langtry
L'eggs/Hanes/Bali
Lenox
London Fog
Manhattan
Multiples
Oneida
OshKosh B'Gosh (The Genuine Article)
Pfaltzgraff
Polly Flinders
Polo/Ralph Lauren
Prestige Fragrance & Cosmetics, PFC Fragrance

Russell Mills, Russell Factory Store
Stone Mountain Handbags
Swank
Totes/Sunglass World
Toys Unlimited
Van Heusen
Warnaco
West Point Pepperell Bed, Bath and Linens Factory Outlet
Credit Cards: Determined by each store
Personal Checks: Determined by each store
Food: Plaza contains a variety of eating establishments
Bus Tours: The center welcomes all bus tours and groups of ten or more. It offers convenient bus parking and driver's lounge, as well as a valuable coupon book to each attendee of scheduled group visits.
Notes or Attractions: Conveniently located directly off I–75 where you will find more than one hundred factory stores, featuring forty-three in the plaza. In addition to shopping, there is an 18-hole golf course and several motels. The center has many special events throughout the year—call for schedule.

Marietta

Rolane Factory Outlet
472 Sessions Street

Directions: From the square in Marietta, go north on Cherokee Street. Go through the 120 loop. Next street is Sessions. Turn left. Store is on right at end of Sessions Street. From I–75, take exit 113 and bear back to the left. Get onto 120 loop. Go to fifth light, turn right onto Cherokee. First street on the left is Sessions.
Phone: (404) 428–2861
Hours: 10:00 A.M.–6:00 P.M., Monday–Saturday; 1:00–6:00 P.M., Sunday
Credit Cards: Discover, MasterCard, Visa
Personal Checks: Yes, with driver's license
Notes or Attractions: Near Atlanta

Morrow

Barry Manufacturing Company
1303 Morrow Industrial Boulevard

Directions: In South Lake Shopping complex
Phone: (404) 968–3966
Hours: 10:00 A.M.–8:00 P.M., Monday–Thursday; 10:00 A.M.–9:00 P.M., Friday; 9:00 A.M.–6:00 P.M., Saturday; 12:30–5:00 P.M., Sunday
Credit Cards: American Express, Discover, MasterCard, Visa
Personal Checks: Yes
Food: Fast food nearby
Bus Tours: Yes

Savannah

Aileen
The Savannah Festival Factory Outlet
11 Gateway Boulevard South, Suite 32

Directions: Intersection of I–95, exit 16, and Route 204 at the outlet center.
Phone: (912) 927–2805
Hours: 9:00 A.M.–9:00 P.M., Monday–Saturday; 11:00 A.M.–6:00 P.M., Sunday
Credit Cards: MasterCard, Visa
Personal Checks: Yes
Food: Fast food and restaurants in the immediate area
Bus Tours: Yes. Ask about a coupon book.
Notes or Attractions: Historic Savannah is fifteen minutes away. Tybee Island is thirty minutes away.

Ribbon Outlet
Savannah Festival Outlet Center

Directions: From I–95, take exit 204 to Highway 204. The outlet is approximately ¼ mile from the exit.
Phone: (912) 927–8499
Hours: 9:00 A.M.–9:00 P.M., Monday–Saturday; 11:00 A.M.–6:00 P.M., Sunday
Credit Cards: MasterCard, Visa
Personal Checks: Yes, with proper identification
Food: Yes, in the immediate area
Bus Tours: Yes

Smyrna

Barry Manufacturing Company
Loehman Plaza
2514 Cobb Parkway

Directions: One mile outside I–285 on Highway 41.
Phone: (404) 859–0366
Hours: 10:00 A.M.–7:00 P.M., Monday–Friday; 9:00 A.M.–6:00 P.M., Saturday; 12:00–5:00 P.M., Sunday
Credit Cards: American Express, Discover, MasterCard, Visa
Personal Checks: Yes
Food: In the area
Bus Tours: Yes
Notes or Attractions: Near Atlanta

Stone Mountain

Barry Manufacturing Company
4879 Memorial Drive

Directions: Inside Rockmore Plaza, off Memorial Drive
Phone: (404) 296–1401
Hours: 10:00 A.M.–8:00 P.M., Monday–Friday; 9:00 A.M.–6:00 P.M., Saturday; 12:30–5:00 P.M., Sunday
Credit Cards: American Express, Discover, MasterCard, Visa
Personal Checks: Yes
Food: Fast food nearby
Bus Tours: Yes

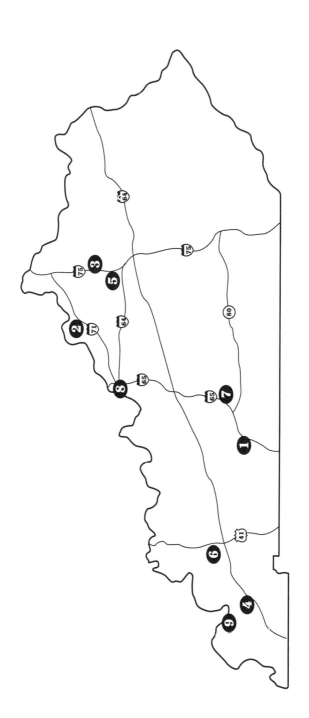

Kentucky

Numbers at the left of this legend correspond to the numbers on the accompanying map. The number to the right of each city's or town's name is the page number on which that municipality's outlets first appear in this book.

Bowling Green

Acme Boot Factory Outlet
2910 Scottsville Road

Directions: Coming from the north on I–65, take exit 22. Turn left at light; go approximately 1 mile, and the outlet is on the right. Coming from the south on I–65, take the first Bowling Green exit, exit 22, and turn right at the light; continue for three stoplights, and the outlet is on the right.
Phone: (615) 552–2000, ext. 267
Hours: 9:00 A.M.–9:00 P.M., Monday–Saturday; 11:00 A.M.–6:00 P.M., Sunday. *Thanksgiving through Christmas:* 9:00 A.M.–10:00 P.M., Monday–Sunday.
Credit Cards: American Express, Discover, MasterCard, Visa
Personal Checks: Yes; both personal and business checks accepted with the proper identification (Acme Boot outlets use Telecheck.)
Food: Several restaurants and fast-food establishments in the area
Bus Tours: Yes
Notes or Attractions: The outlet is approximately 30 miles south of Mammoth Cave and 45 miles from Opryland. A large shopping mall is across the street; another clothing outlet and a towel-and-bedding outlet are about 1 mile away. You can drive about ten minutes north to the Corvette plant.

Carrollton

VF Factory Outlet
R.R. 3, Highway 227

Directions: Approximately 1 mile from I–71, on the right.
Phone: (502) 732–6666
Hours: 9:00 A.M.–7:00 P.M., Monday–Thursday; 9:00 A.M.–9:00 P.M., Friday–Saturday; 12:00–5:00 P.M., Sunday; some seasonal variations
Credit Cards: Discover, MasterCard, Visa
Personal Checks: Yes
ATM: Yes

Food: Fast food in the immediate area
Bus Tours: Yes, with a gift for the driver and tour director
Notes or Attractions: General Butler State Park 1 mile away

Dry Ridge

Ribbon Outlet
Dry Ridge Outlet Center

Directions: From I–75, take Dry Ridge exit. When you come to the blinking light (if from the south), make a right turn. If coming from the north, take a left turn. Outlet is on the right.
Phone: (606) 824–9516
Hours: Call for information
Credit Cards: MasterCard, Visa
Personal Checks: Yes, with the proper identification
Food: Yes, within the immediate area
Bus Tours: Yes

Eddyville

West Kentucky Factory Outlets
208 Outlet Avenue

Directions: Interstate 24 to exit 40, then east 2¾ miles on right on U.S. 641/62; or take the West Kentucky Parkway exit 4, then west 3 miles on U.S. 641/62 on the left.
Phone: (502) 388–7379
Hours: *January–March:* 9:00 A.M.–7:00 P.M., Monday–Saturday; 12:00–5:00 P.M., Sunday. *April–December:* 9:00 A.M.–9:00 P.M., Monday–Saturday; 11:00 A.M.–7:00 P.M., Sunday.
Outlets:
Aileen
Arrow Factory Store
Barbizon Lingerie
Bass Shoes

Black & Decker
Bon Worth
Book Warehouse
Boston Traders
Brass Factory
Brown Shoe Co.
Bugle Boy
Corning Revere
Damon/Enro
Dress Ups!
Etienne Aigner
Florsheim Shoe
Full Size Fashions
Hush Puppies
Izod
Jaymar
Jonathan Logan
Kitchen Collection
L'eggs/Hanes/Bali
Libbey Glass
London Fog
Nike/Sports Outlet/Reebok
Oneida
OshKosh B'Gosh (The Genuine Article)
Paper Factory
Polo/Ralph Lauren
Prestige Fragrance & Cosmetics, PFC Fragrance
Ribbon Outlet
S & K Menswear
Socks Galore and More
Swank
Sweatshirt Co.
Toy Liquidators
Van Heusen
Wallet Works
Walnut Bowls/Chicago Cutlery
Welcome Home
Westport

Credit Cards: American Express, Diners Club, Discover, MasterCard, Visa
Personal Checks: Yes, stores require two types of identification
ATM: Yes, at branch bank on mall property by entrance
Additional Savings: Sidewalk Sales, first weekend of each month; Nine Day Sidewalk Sale, late July–early August
Food: Yes
Bus Tours: Yes. Discount coupon sheets for all passengers, food coupons for driver and guide. (Pick up coupons and unload passengers at Welcome Center; coupon sheets may be mailed to tour operator in advance.)
Notes and Attractions: Kentucky's largest outdoor recreation area includes Lake Barkley, Kentucky Lake, and Land Between The Lakes National Recreation Area. Near National Quilt Museum in Paducah and National Boy Scout Museum in Murray. Fishing, boating, waterslides, and sightseeing abound!

Georgetown

Factory Stores of America
401 Commercial Drive

Directions: Traveling I–75, take exit 125 or 126 just north of Lexington, Kentucky; the outlet center is visible from these exits.
Phone: (502) 863–3660; (800) SHOP–USA
Hours: 9:00 A.M.–9:00 P.M., Monday–Saturday; 1:00–6:00 P.M., Sunday; closed Christmas Day and Easter Sunday
Outlets:
Aileen
Banister Shoes
Bass Shoes
Black & Decker
Bon Worth
Book Warehouse
Boot Factory
Bugle Boy

Carolina Pottery
Corning Revere
Duck Head
Factory Linens
Jockey
Le Creuset
Levi's
$9.99 Stockroom
Paper Factory
Polly Flinders
Prestige Fragrance & Cosmetics, PFC Fragrance
Ribbon Outlet
Socks Galore and More
Stone Mountain Handbags
Totes/Sunglass World
Toy Liquidators
Van Heusen
Westport

Credit Cards: American Express, MasterCard, Visa

Personal Checks: Varies by merchant

Additional Savings: Special sales are offered throughout the year. Many of the outlets offer weekly sales. There a sale of some kind at Factory Stores of America 363 days a year.

Food: Food court on the premises

Bus Tours: Yes, during outlet center hours. Coaches drive up to Factory Stores of America, where they'll be greeted. Groups receive discount coupon booklets redeemable throughout the center. Escorts receive $10.00 gift certificates and $5.00 food vouchers.

Notes or Attractions: Located in the midst of Bluegrass Country—the Kentucky Horse Park is located 1½ miles from the outlet center, as is the American Saddle Horse Museum. Many historic sites in the immediate area. Within one-half hour, the Lexington Children's Museum. The Toyota Manufacturing USA plant, five minutes from the outlet center, offers free tours on Tuesday and Thursday.

Hanson

Factory Stores of America
100 Factory Outlet Drive

Directions: Pennyrile Parkway North, exit 45 at Madisonville, U.S. 41 North, right on Highway 260.
Phone: (502) 322–8480
Hours: *January–October:* 9:00 A.M.–7:00 P.M., Monday–Thursday; 9:00 A.M.–9:00 P.M., Friday–Saturday; 12:00–5:00 P.M., Sunday. *November–December:* 9:00 A.M.–8:00 P.M., Monday–Thursday; 9:00 A.M.–9:00 P.M., Friday–Saturday; 12:00–5:30 P.M., Sunday.
Outlets:
Banister Shoes
Prestige Fragrance & Cosmetics, PFC Fragrance
Van Heusen
Vanity Fair
Credit Cards: Discover, MasterCard, Visa
Personal Checks: Yes; driver's license required
Food: Restaurants and fast food within 5 miles
Bus Tours: Yes; free lunch to drivers
Notes or Attractions: State parks with historical downtown tour. In nearby Eddyville, there is the Eddyville Outlet Center.

Horse Cave

Jent Factory Outlets
846 Flint Ridge Road

Directions: The center is clearly visible from I–65 at exit 58.
Phone: (502) 786–4446
Hours: *January–March:* 9:00 A.M.–7:00 P.M., Monday–Saturday; 11:00 A.M.–5:00 P.M. Sunday. *April–December:* 9:00 A.M.–9:00 P.M., Monday–Saturday; 11:00 A.M.–7:00 P.M. Sunday. Closed at 6:00 P.M. Thanksgiving, Christmas, and New Year's Eves. Closed Thanksgiving and Christmas Days.

Outlets:
Aileen
Amity
Arrow Factory Store
Banister Shoes
Book Warehouse
Brass Factory
Bugle Boy
Corning Revere
Dress Ups!
Florsheim Shoe
Fruit of the Loom
Izod
Jaymar
Kitchen Collection
Libbey Glass
London Fog
OshKosh B'Gosh (The Genuine Article)
Paper Factory
Prestige Fragrance & Cosmetics, PFC Fragrance
Ribbon Outlet
Socks Galore & More
Sports Outlet
Toy Liquidators
Welcome Home
Credit Cards: American Express, Discover, MasterCard, Visa
Personal Checks: Yes, most stores require two forms of identification
Additional Savings: Every Tuesday is Senior Citizens Day, with an additional 10 percent off at participating stores. Mailing lists kept at individual stores.
Food: Fast food nearby
Bus Tours: Yes, discount coupons are available.
Notes or Attractions: Central Kentucky's Cave Area; across I–65 from Kentucky Down Under Australian Theme Park and Mammoth Onyx Cave; 10 miles from Mammoth Cave National Park; 35 miles from Bowling Green; 75 miles from Louisville

Louisville

Acme Boot Factory Outlet
3299 Fern Valley Road

Directions: From I–65, take the Fern Valley Road exit. The outlet is approximately 2 miles on the left.
Phone: (615) 552–2000, ext. 267
Hours: 9:00 A.M.–9:00 P.M., Monday–Saturday; 12:00–6:00 P.M., Sunday. Hours are extended during the Thanksgiving and Christmas holiday period.
Credit Cards: American Express, Discover, MasterCard, Visa
Personal Checks: Yes, with valid driver's license or other identification
Food: Restaurants and fast-food establishments in the immediate area
Bus Tours: Yes
Notes or Attractions: Louisville is home of the Kentucky Derby.

Paducah

Acme Boot
3790 Hinkleville Road

Directions: From I–24, take the Wickliff/Paducah exit, exit 4, Highway 60 west. Outlet is ½ mile on the right.
Phone: (615) 552–2000, ext. 267
Hours: 9:00 A.M.–9:00 P.M., Monday–Saturday; 11:00 A.M.–6:00 P.M., Sunday
Credit Cards: American Express, Discover, MasterCard, Visa
Personal Checks: Yes, with valid driver's license or other identification
Food: Restaurants and fast-food establishments in the immediate area
Bus Tours: Yes
Notes or Attractions: Bluegrass Downs Horse Track 2 miles away

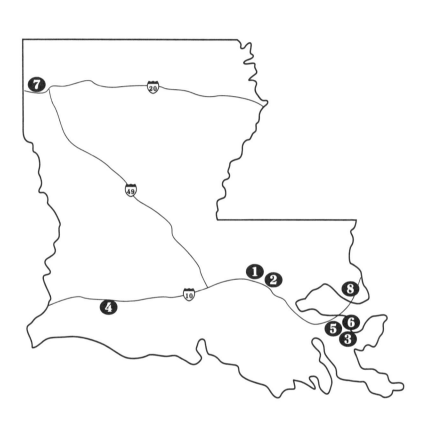

Louisiana

Numbers at the left of this legend correspond to the numbers on the accompanying map. The number to the right of each city's or town's name is the page number on which that municipality's outlets first appear in this book.

Baton Rouge

Barry Manufacturing Company
9505 Airline Highway

Directions: Outlet is near I–10.
Phone: (504) 923–2266
Hours: 9:00 A.M.–8:00 P.M., Monday–Friday; 9:00 A.M.–6:00 P.M., Saturday; 12:00–5:00 P.M., Sunday
Credit Cards: American Express, Discover, MasterCard, Visa
Personal Checks: Yes
Food: Fast food nearby
Bus Tours: Yes
Notes or Attractions: Near historic area

Gonzales

Aileen
Tanger Factory Outlet Center
2200 Tanger Boulevard, Suite 1

Directions: I–10, exit 177; intersects with Highway 30, Tanger Boulevard
Phone: (504) 647–4350
Hours: 10:00 A.M.–9:00 P.M., Monday–Saturday; 12:00–6:00 P.M., Sunday
Credit Cards: MasterCard, Visa
Personal Checks: Yes
Food: Vending machines and sandwiches
Bus Tours: Yes. Ask about coupon books.

Gretna

Barry Manufacturing Company
95-C West Bank Expressway

Directions: Located on West Bank Expressway
Phone: (504) 362–0181
Hours: 9:00 A.M.–8:00 P.M., Monday and Thursday; 9:00 A.M.–6:00 P.M., Tuesday, Wednesday, Friday, Saturday; 12:00–5:00 P.M., Sunday
Credit Cards: American Express, Discover, MasterCard, Visa
Personal Checks: Yes
Food: Nearby
Bus Tours: Yes
Notes or Attractions: Within an easy drive of New Orleans

Iowa

Vanity Fair Outlet
800 Factory Outlet Drive

Directions: From I–10, take exit 43 for city of Iowa. Go to the light and take a left onto Miller Road. The outlet is approximately ½ mile on the left.
Phone: (318) 582–3568
Hours: 9:00 A.M.–9:00 P.M., Monday–Saturday; 12:00–6:00 P.M., Sunday
Credit Cards: Discover, MasterCard, Visa
Personal Checks: Yes
ATM: Yes, located in the mall hallway next to the deli
Food: In the area or nearby
Bus Tours: Yes; discount coupons to the tour bus upon arrival

Kenner

Barry Manufacturing Company
2647 Williams Boulevard

Directions: Near the airport
Phone: (504) 466–0014
Hours: 9:00 A.M.–9:00 P.M., Monday–Friday; 9:00 A.M.–6:00 P.M., Saturday; 12:00–5:00 P.M., Sunday
Credit Cards: American Express, Discover, MasterCard, Visa
Personal Checks: Yes, in-state only
Food: Fast food nearby
Bus Tours: Yes

New Orleans

Barry Manufacturing Company
7300 Read Boulevard

Directions: Read Boulevard is just off I–10.
Phone: (504) 241–9033
Hours: 9:00 A.M.–9:00 P.M., Monday–Friday; 9:00 A.M.–6:00 P.M., Saturday; 12:00–5:00 P.M., Sunday
Credit Cards: American Express, Discover, MasterCard, Visa
Personal Checks: Yes
Food: Nearby
Bus Tours: Yes
Notes or Attractions: All the excitement of New Orleans!

Dansk Factory Outlet
French Quarter
541 Royal Street

Directions: Take I–10 east to Vieux Carre exit. Left at light. Straight through next light. Follow signs via Toulouse.
Phone: (504) 522–0482
Hours: 10:00 A.M.–6:00 P.M., Monday–Sunday
Credit Cards: MasterCard, Visa
Personal Checks: Yes
ATM: 1½ blocks away
Food: Nearby
Bus Tours: Yes
Alternate Transportation: Taxi service
Notes or Attractions: Bourbon Street 1 block away

Shreveport

Libbey Glass Factory Outlet
4302 Jewella and I–20

Directions: Exit 14 off I–20
Phone: (318) 631–0367
Hours: *June–December:*10:00 A.M.–5:00 P.M., Monday–Saturday; 1:00–5:00 P.M., Sunday
Credit Cards: Discover, MasterCard, Visa
Personal Checks: Yes, with driver's license or proper identification
Additional Savings: Tent Sale, July; weekend after Thanksgiving
Food: Fast food within ½ mile; cafeteria eight minutes from outlet; great food within fifteen minutes
Bus Tours: Yes; special parking available; gift for the tour director or bus driver
Notes or Attractions: This is a sportsman's paradise. The Shreveport Museum is five minutes away. Cross Lake (Watertown) is open during the summer. Riverboat gambling begins in 1994.

Slidell

Slidell Factory Stores
1000 Caruso Boulevard

Directions: Just 20 miles east of New Orleans on I–10 at exit 263
Phone: (504) 646–0756
Hours: 9:00 A.M.–9:00 P.M., Monday–Saturday; 12:30–5:30 P.M., Sunday
Outlets:
Aileen
American Tourister
Arrow Factory Store
Banister Shoes
Bass Shoes
Bon Worth
Book Factory
Boots, Etc
Bruce Alan Bags
Bugle Boy
Cape Isle Knitters
Corning Revere
Designer Silks, Etc.
Eagle's Eye
Factory Connection
Famous Footwear
Florsheim Shoe
Full Size Fashion
Jerzees
Jordache
Kelly's Kids
Kid's Collection
Kitchen Collection
Leather Loft
L'eggs/Hanes/Bali
Levi's
Libbey Glass Factory Outlet
Lingerie Shoppe
Oneida

Paper Factory
Perfumania
Rack Room Shoes
Ribbon Outlet
S & K Menswear
Sequins Originals
Stone Mountain Handbags
Swank
Van Heusen
Wallet Works
Welcome Home
WEMCO/Wembley Factory Store
West Point Pepperell
Westport
Credit Cards: American Express, Discover, MasterCard, Visa
Personal Checks: Yes
Food: The Yogurt Shoppe and various fast-food establishments
Bus Tours: Yes. Tour-bus drivers who park at the Slidell Factory Stores will receive coupons to distribute to all shoppers in their buses. In addition, each tour-bus driver and host will receive certificates for a variety of free gifts. If possible, tour-bus operators or tour organizers should contact the Slidell Factory Stores before the planned arrival date.
Notes or Attractions: Swamp tours; Antiques District

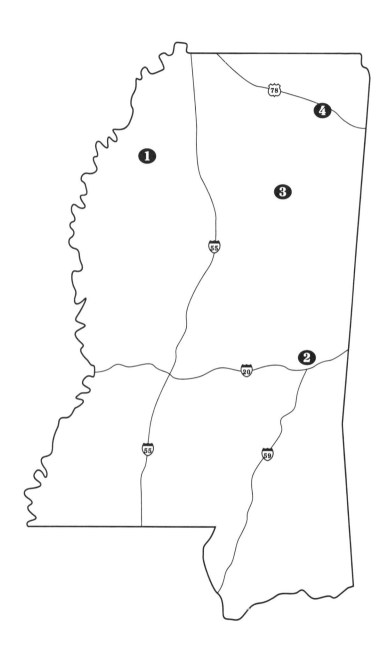

Mississippi

Numbers at the left of this legend correspond to the numbers on the accompanying map. The number to the right of each city's or town's name is the page number on which that municipality's outlets first appear in this book.

1. Clarksdale, 150
2. Meridian, 150

3. Sturgis, 151
4. Tupelo, 151

Clarksdale

Allan's Fashion Outlet
233 Yazoo Avenue

Directions: Heading south from Memphis, Tennessee, take Highway 61
to Clarksdale (located west of I–55)
Phone: (601) 624–4741
Hours: 9:30 A.M.–5:30 P.M., Monday–Saturday
Credit Cards: MasterCard, Visa
Personal Checks: Yes, with proper identification
Food: Within driving distance
Bus Tours: Yes
Notes or Attractions: Blues Museum nearby

Meridian

Outlet Unlimited
2218 4th Street

Directions: From I–20, take the 22nd Avenue exit and go downtown
until you reach 4th Street. Turn left, and the outlet is the first business
on the right.
Phone: (601) 485–7814
Hours: 9:00 A.M.–5:00 P.M., Monday–Saturday
Credit Cards: Discover, MasterCard, Visa
Personal Checks: In-state only
Food: Historic restaurant near the outlet location
Bus Tours: Yes
Notes or Attractions: Many people come here just to eat at the historic
restaurant in the downtown section of Meridian where the Old Opera
House is located. Near this business is the Jimmy Rodgers Museum.
There is also Dunn's Falls, Okatibbee Lake, and the Frank Cockran Cen-
ter, which offers craft shows twice a month.

Sturgis

The Merchandise Warehouse
Highway 12

Directions: Located on Highway 12 in downtown Sturgis, 13 miles due west of Starkville
Phone: (601) 465–6008
Hours: *January–September:* 9:30 A.M.–5:30 P.M., Thursday, Friday, Saturday. *October–December:* 9:30 A.M.–5:30 P.M., Monday–Saturday.
Credit Cards: MasterCard, Visa
Personal Checks: Yes, with a valid telephone number and driver's license
Food: Cafe nearby
Bus Tours: Yes; 10 percent discount and plenty of parking
Notes or Attractions: Mississippi State University is 14 miles west of the outlet on Highway 12.

Tupelo

VF Factory Outlet
423 Eason Boulevard

Directions: From U.S. Highway 45, take U.S. Highway 78 east to Eason Boulevard for approximately ½ mile.
Phone: (601) 844–5890
Hours: 9:00 A.M.–7:00 P.M., Monday–Thursday; 9:00 A.M.–9:00 P.M., Friday–Saturday; 12:00–5:30 P.M., Sunday
Credit Cards: Discover, MasterCard, Visa
Personal Checks: Yes, with proper identification
ATM: Yes, within 2 miles of mall
Food: Soda and snacks available on-site
Bus Tours: All first-time bus drivers receive a free pair of Lee jeans with tour groups of twenty or more.
Notes or Attractions: Within 3 miles of the Elvis Presley birthplace park and historical downtown Tupelo

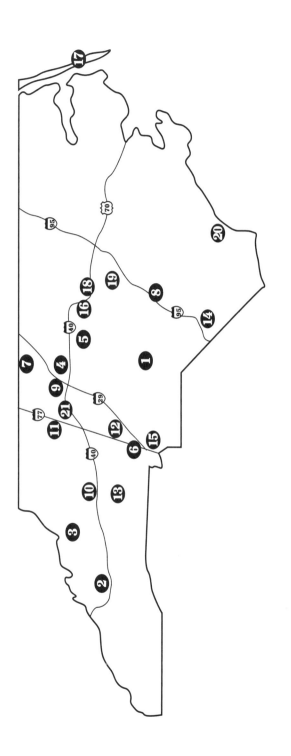

North Carolina

Numbers at the left of this legend correspond to the numbers on the accompanying map. The number to the right of each city's or town's name is the page number on which that municipality's outlets first appear in this book.

Special Note: North Carolina is known for its furniture industry. More than 60 percent of all the furniture made in the United States is made in North Carolina. The state has so many furniture outlets, each offering its own distinctive style and quality, that the conscientious shopper would be wise to prepare for a trip to this part of the South. To assist in the selection process, write for the following publications:

1. Furniture: We've Got It Made in Hickory!
Catawba County Chamber of Commerce
P.O. Box 1828
Hickory, North Carolina 28603
Provided by the Catawba County Chamber of Commerce, this free booklet gives an overview of the Hickory-area furniture heritage and of selected retailers, motels, and stores. Expect as much as a 50 percent savings (and sometimes more) buying directly from this area of "furniture country."

2. The North Carolina Furniture Guide
Carolina Publications, Inc.
P.O. Box 2550
Greensboro, North Carolina 27402
This 32-page publication covers furniture shopping in Greensboro, Wilmington, Raleigh/Smithfield/Richlands, Troy, Reidsville, Black Mountain, Winston-Salem/Kannapolis, Hickory, High Point/Thomasville/Denton, Forest City, Boone/Patterson, Statesville, and Mt. Airy. (**Note:** There is a $3.00 charge for this publication.)

Warning: If you haven't done research prior to your trip, don't be fooled by signs that read "% off." Ask what the percentage is deducted from—wholesale, retail, or factory price. Also know what your favorite style retails for before you try to make a deal.

Aberdeen

Century Curtain and Bedding Outlet
301 Fields Drive
Sandhills Industrial Park

Directions: Route 1 east to Highway 5. (Located between Aberdeen and Pinehurst.) Turn left on Highway 5 just past Aberdeen Carpet Mill.
Hours: 9:00 A.M.–4:00 P.M., Monday–Saturday
Credit Cards: MasterCard, Visa
Personal Checks: Yes
Food: Nearby
Bus Tours: Yes
Notes or Attractions: Near Aberdeen Lake

Rolane Factory Outlet
Sandhills Shopping Center
U.S. Highway 1 North

Directions: From Pinehurst, take Highway 15/510 North to U.S. Highway 1 North. Outlet center is on the right.
Phone: (919) 226–5887
Hours: 10:00 A.M.–7:00 P.M., Monday–Saturday; 1:00–6:00 P.M., Sunday
Credit Cards: Discover, MasterCard, Visa
Personal Checks: Yes, with valid driver's license
Food: Restaurants nearby
Notes or Attractions: Near Pinehurst Country Club and other golf resorts

Asheville

Hamrick's of Asheville
River Ridge Outlet Center
800 Fairview Road

Directions: Take I–40 to exit 53B (I–240), then I–240 to exit 8

Phone: (704) 298–6400
Hours: 10:00 A.M.–9:00 P.M., Monday–Saturday
Credit Cards: Discover, MasterCard, Visa
Personal Checks: Yes, with valid driver's license
Bus Tours: Yes, bus driver and one host will receive $15 off total purchase with thirteen or more passengers. All bus passengers will receive a free gift.
Food: Yes, six restaurants in immediate area

Blowing Rock

Duck Head Outlet Store
Shoppes on the Parkway
Highway 321 North

Directions: Right on Highway 321, Suite 26
Phone: (704) 295–3819
Hours: *January–March:* 10:00 A.M.–6:00 P.M., Monday–Saturday; 1:00–6:00 P.M., Sunday. *April–December:* 10:00 A.M.–9:00 P.M., Monday–Saturday; 1:00–6:00 P.M., Sunday.
Credit Cards: Discover, MasterCard, Visa
Personal Checks: Yes, with driver's license or picture identification
Additional Savings: Two inventory sales (last week of December and last week of June)
Food: Yes, in vicinity
Bus Tours: Yes
Notes or Attractions: Within one of the most beautiful mountain/ tourist areas in North Carolina

Shoppes on the Parkway
Highway 321

Directions: Highway 321 and 321 Bypass
Phone: (704) 295–4248
Hours: *January–March:* 10:00 A.M.–6:00 P.M., Monday–Saturday; 1:00–6:00 P.M., Sunday. *April–December:* 10:00 A.M.–9:00 P.M., Monday–Saturday; 1:00–6:00 P.M., Sunday.
Outlets:
Adolfo II
Aileen
Anne Klein
Arrow Factory Store
Banister Shoes
Bass Shoes
Boston Trader Kids
Bruce Alan Bags
Cape Isle Knitters
Champion-Hanes
Corning Revere
Duck Head
Evan Picone
Gilligan & O'Malley
Jones New York
Necklace Factory
Prestige Fragrance & Cosmetics, PFC Fragrance
Ribbon Outlet
Royal Doulton
Socks Galore and More
Tie One On
Toy Liquidators
Van Heusen
Welcome Home
Westport
Credit Cards: Varies from store to store
Personal Checks: Varies from store to store
Food: Yes, fast food
Bus Tours: Yes

Burlington

Burlington Manufacturers Outlet Center
2389 Corporation Parkway

Directions: Take I–85 to exit 145; the center is clearly visible from I–85.
Phone: (919) 227–2872
Hours: *January–February:* 10:00 A.M.–6:00 P.M. *March–December:* 10:00 A.M.–9:00 P.M. Closed Easter Sunday, Thanksgiving Day, and Christmas Day.
Outlets:

Adolfo II
Aileen
Allen Edmonds
American Tourister
Avon Fashions
Barbizon Lingerie
Barett Shoes
Bass Shoes
Black & Decker
Bon Worth
Book Annex
Brown Shoe Co.
Bugle Boy
Burlington Artists League Gallery
Burlington Brands
Burlington Coat Factory Outlet
Burlington Shoe
Carter's
Casual Male Big and Tall
Champion-Hanes
Dixie Belle Lingerie
Donnkenny
Dress Barn
Dress Barn Woman

Eagle's Eye
Eagle's Eye Kids
Famous Brands Housewares
Famous Footwear
Farberware, Inc.
Finish Line
Hamilton Luggage and Handbags
Hanes Mill
Hit or Miss
Izod
Keith's Record Shop
Le Creuset
Leslie Fay
Linens 'n Things
Liz Claiborne Irregulars Only
London Fog
Maidenform
Mikasa
9 West
Paper Factory
Piece Goods
Prestige Fragrance & Cosmetics,
    PFC Fragrance
Princess Handbags

Rack Room Shoes
S & K Menswear
Scent Saver
Shoe Show
Sneakee Feet
Sweater Shops

Toy Liquidators
Uniform/Lingerie Connection
Van Heusen
Variety Crafts
West Point Pepperell Bed, Bath
   and Linens Factory Outlet

> Due to corporate restrictions as outlined by this outlet mall, the publisher has been unable to provide profiles on the following outlets. These outlets also have been omitted from the indexes.

Ashtin Jewelry
Bridal Mart
Casualwear Express
Children's Wear
Diamond P. Western
Garment District
Plej's
Simply Six
Stetson

Credit Cards: American Express, MasterCard, Visa (and Discover at some stores)

Personal Checks: Yes, with the proper identification—usually a valid driver's license and one credit card

Food: Three restaurants on-site and five surrounding the center

Bus Tours: Yes. The Welcome Center has a bus representative on weekends to greet shoppers and supply them with a complimentary shopping bag and coupon booklet. (Casualwear Express handles this function on weekdays.) Free parking.

Notes or Attractions: Burlington has more than a hundred outlets, with this facility housing many of those. City Park has an original, restored Dentzel carousel. For children, there is a roller-skating rink in the area; City Park has kiddie rides and a minitrain. North Carolina Zoological Park (in Asheboro) is about forty minutes away. Tram service is free to shuttle around the center's twenty-two acres on weekends.

Rolane Factory Outlet
Burlington Outlet Mall
2589 Eric Lane, Store 124

Directions: Take exit 43 off I–84, about 3 miles west of Burlington.
Phone: (919) 226–5887
Hours: 9:00 A.M.–9:00 P.M., Monday–Saturday; 1:00–6:00 P.M., Sunday
Credit Cards: Discover, MasterCard, Visa
Personal Checks: Yes, with valid driver's license
Food: Yes
Bus Tours: Yes
Alternate Transportation: Taxi service from Burlington
Notes or Attractions: Burlington has the largest concentration of outlet
centers in North Carolina.

Chapel Hill

Rolane Factory Outlet
105 Rams Plaza

Phone: (919) 942–6552
Credit Cards: Discover, MasterCard, Visa
Personal Checks: Yes, with driver's license
Food: In the immediate area
Notes or Attractions: Located in the city that's home to the University
of North Carolina

Charlotte

Barry Manufacturing Company
4035 South Boulevard

Directions: South Boulevard runs parallel to I–77. Take the Woodlawn
Road exit and turn right onto South Boulevard.
Phone: (704) 525–6635

Hours: 9:00 A.M.–9:00 P.M., Monday, Thursday, Friday; 9:00 A.M.–6:00 P.M., Tuesday, Wednesday, Saturday; 12:00–5:00 P.M., Sunday
Credit Cards: American Express, Discover, MasterCard, Visa
Personal Checks: Yes
Food: Fast food nearby
Bus Tours: Yes
Notes or Attractions: Carowinds Theme Park nearby

Eden

Rolane Factory Outlet
415 South Van Buren Road

Directions: From Highway 29, take Route 14 south toward Eden. Store is on Route 14.
Phone: (919) 623–6516
Hours: 10:00 A.M.–8:00 P.M., Monday–Saturday; 1:00–6:00 P.M., Sunday
Credit Cards: Discover, MasterCard, Visa
Personal Checks: Yes, with driver's license

Fayetteville

Hamrick's of Fayetteville
Marketfair
1916 Skibo Road

Directions: Take Highway 74 to Highway 401 onto Skibo Road.
Phone: (919) 868–6255
Hours: 10:00 A.M.–9:00 P.M., Monday–Saturday
Credit Cards: Discover, MasterCard, Visa
Personal Checks: Yes, with valid driver's license
Food: Available in the immediate area
Bus Tours: Yes. Bus driver and one host receive $15 off total purchase with thirteen or more passengers. All bus passengers receive a free gift.

Greensboro

Barry Manufacturing Company
2614 High Point Road

Directions: Take the High Point Road exit off I–40.
Phone: (919) 852–2665
Hours: 9:00 A.M.–6:00 P.M., Monday–Saturday (until 9:00 P.M. Friday); 12:00–5:00 P.M., Sunday
Credit Cards: American Express, Discover, MasterCard, Visa
Personal Checks: Yes
Food: Fast food nearby
Bus Tours: Yes

Rolane Factory Outlet
1006 Howard Street

Directions: I–40, take Coliseum exit. Follow signs toward Coliseum. Left at Patterson Avenue. Right at Holden Road. Right at Spring Garden. Right at Howard Street.
Phone: (919) 299–8831
Hours: 10:00 A.M.–9:00 P.M., Monday–Saturday; 1:00–6:00 P.M., Sunday
Credit Cards: Discover, MasterCard, Visa
Personal Checks: Yes, with driver's license
Notes or Attractions: One of the oldest and largest factory-owned stores in the South. Still located in the old hosiery mill.

Hickory

Hamrick's of Hickory
Catawba Mall
Highway 70 SW

Directions: Take Highway 127 toward Hickory; then take exit for Highway 70 and 321 South. Bear right off the exit onto Highway 70 E. At third light turn right into Catawba Mall. Hamrick's is straight ahead.

Phone: (704) 322–4642
Hours: 9:00 A.M.–7:00 P.M., Monday–Saturday
Credit Cards: Discover, MasterCard, Visa
Personal Checks: Yes, with valid driver's license
Food: Available in immediate area
Bus Tours: Yes. Bus driver and one host receive $15 off total purchase with thirteen or more passengers. All bus passengers receive a free gift.

Hickory Oriental Rug Gallery
Startown Plaza
2019 Highway 70 SE

Directions: Take exit 125 off I–40; go south to the second light, turn left on Highway 70, and proceed a half mile. Turn left by Burger King restaurant. The plaza, on the left, is directly across from Valley Hills Mall.
Phone: (704) 327–7847
Hours: 10:00 A.M.–8:00 P.M., Monday–Friday; 10:00 A.M.–7:00 P.M., Saturday; 1:00–6:00 P.M., Sunday
Credit Cards: No
Personal Checks: Yes, with valid driver's license, work phone number, and major credit card
ATM: Two blocks away at local bank
Food: Fast-food establishments and restaurants in the immediate area
Bus Tours: Yes, with advance notice. Will conduct a free class on oriental rugs for groups of ten or more.
Alternate Transportation: Regional airport is fifteen minutes away. Outlet will pick up customers at airport with prior notice.
Notes or Attractions: A regional shopping center is across the street; movie theaters, an art museum, and a science center are close by. Two miles away is auto racing on weekends, and mountain resorts are within a forty-five-minute drive. This area is the "hub" of furniture outlets. North Carolina's largest furniture mart is within 200 feet.

Rolane Factory Outlet
2151 North Center Street

Directions: From I–40, take Lenoir Rhyne Boulevard to Highway 127 North. Store is off Highway 127 North on left side in small strip center.
Phone: (704) 328–3251
Credit Cards: Discover, MasterCard, Visa
Personal Checks: Yes, with driver's license
Food: Restaurant is located within the center.
Notes or Attractions: Hickory is home to Hickory Furniture Mart, the world's largest furniture outlet.

Jonesville

Chatham Country Store Outlet
Riverview Village Shopping Center
Route 1, Box 1057, Highway 67

Directions: From I–77, take exit 82 toward Elkin. Outlet is within sight of I–77.
Phone: (919) 835–3306
Hours: 9:00 A.M.–6:00 P.M., Monday–Saturday; 1:00–5:00 P.M., Sunday (later hours during holidays, especially November and December)
Credit Cards: MasterCard, Visa
Personal Checks: Yes, with valid driver's license
Food: Huddle House, Shoney's, McDonalds, Wendy's
Bus Tours: Yes
Notes or Attractions: Not far from the beautiful Blue Ridge Mountains

Kannapolis

Cannon Village
200 West Avenue

Directions: From Charlotte: Drive north thirty minutes on I–85, take Kannapolis exit 58 or exit 63 and follow the signs to Cannon Village.
Phone: (704) 938–3200
Hours: *January–March:* 9:00 A.M.–8:00 P.M., Monday–Saturday; 1:00–6:00 P.M., Sunday. *April–October:* 9:00 A.M.–8:00 P.M., Monday–Saturday; 1:00–6:00 P.M., Sunday. *Thanksgiving–Christmas:* 9:00 A.M.–10:00 P.M., Monday–Saturday; 1:00–6:00 P.M., Sunday.
Outlets:
Aileen Factory Outlet
Anne's Dress Shop
Balloons Unlimited
Bass Shoes
Beacon Blanket Boutique
Bon Worth
Brass Exchange
Cannon Bed & Bath Outlet
Cannon Village Antique Mall
Carolina Interiors
Carter's
Churchill's
Clothing Warehouse
Designer Desk
Dress Barn
Fall's Custom-Jewelry
Footprints
Gift Corner
Hamilton Luggage and Handbags
Hats Etc.
Kitchen Collection
K-Town Furniture
L'eggs/Hanes/Bali
London Fog
Paper Factory

Phidippides
Southern Charm
Uncommon Scents
Van Heusen
Village Books
Village Boutique
Village Frame Shop
Village Furniture House
Virginia's
Waccamaw Pottery
Credit Cards: American Express, Discover, MasterCard, Visa (in most stores)
Personal Checks: Usually, with two forms of identification
ATM: Yes
Food: Cafeteria, fast-food kiosks, ice-cream parlor, doughnut shop, sandwich shop, restaurant
Bus Tours: Yes—members of the National Tour Association, Inc., and the American Bus Association. Contact the Cannon Village Visitor's Center. Discount coupons for members of tour groups. Gift certificates and complimentary meals for tour operator and driver.
Notes or Attractions: Ample parking. Free guided tours of the Fieldcrest/Cannon Manufacturing Plant are available on a limited basis. Ambience of the colonial era. Playground for children nearby. Wednesday is senior citizen's day.

Rolane Factory Outlet
928 Cloverleaf Plaza

Directions: From I–85, take exit 36. Follow signs to Kannapolis. Entrance to Cloverleaf Plaza is on the right, about 200 yards from the interstate.
Phone: (704) 786–5214
Hours: 10:00 A.M.–8:00 P.M., Monday–Friday; 10:00 A.M.–6:00 P.M., Saturday; 1:00–6:00 P.M., Sunday
Credit Cards: Discover, MasterCard, Visa
Personal Checks: Yes, with driver's license
Food: Restaurants in the center

Lincolnton

Rolane Factory Outlet
Highway 321, Bypass North

Phone: (704) 735–0616
Credit Cards: Discover, MasterCard, Visa
Personal Checks: Yes, with driver's license
Food: Available nearby

Lumberton

The Lumberton Outlet Center
3431 Lackey Street

Directions: Located at exit 20 off I–95, 20 miles north of the North and South Carolina border
Phone: (919) 739–9999
Hours: 9:00 A.M.–9:00 P.M., Monday–Saturday; 1:00–6:00 P.M., Sunday
Outlets:
Bass Shoes
Cigarette-Magazine Outlet
Converse Shoe
Golf Outlet
Lumberton Outlet Flea Market
Piece Goods
Rack Room Shoes
Rolane Factory Outlet
Smithy's Gifts & Lingerie
Van Heusen
West Point Pepperell Bed, Bath and Linens Factory Outlet
Credit Cards: Varies by store
Personal Checks: Yes
Food: Three restaurants serve all types of American food for breakfast, lunch, and dinner. A Chinese buffet is also available.
Bus Tours: Yes

Notes or Attractions: The Lumberton Visitors Center is located in the outlet center. In the area you can play golf or tennis; canoe the Lumber River; stroll through the historic downtown area or the Springtime Dogwood Trail and the Flora McDonald Gardens; tour industrial facilities or attend an auction at one of the many tobacco markets; or tour the American Indian Museum. Call the Lumberton Visitors Center at (919) 739–9999 for information about the sixteen motels and forty-seven restaurants at this exit.

Matthews

Hamrick's of Matthews
Windsor Square
9609 E. Independence Boulevard

Directions: Take I–85 north or south, then take Highway 74E into Charlotte. Stay on Highway 74E through Charlotte city limits. Hamrick's is located on the left at Windsor Square.
Phone: (704) 847–1019
Hours: 9:00 A.M.–8:00 P.M., Monday–Saturday
Credit Cards: Discover, MasterCard, Visa
Personal Checks: Yes, with valid driver's license
Food: Available in immediate area
Bus Tours: Yes. Bus driver and one host receive $15 off total purchase with thirteen or more passengers. All bus passengers receive a free gift.

Home Fashions Outlet
1280 W. John Street

Directions: Head south from Charlotte on Old Monroe Road. W. John Street is off Old Monroe Road.
Phone: (704) 847–1512
Hours: 9:00 A.M.–4:00 P.M., Monday–Saturday
Credit Cards: MasterCard, Visa
Personal Checks: Yes
Food: Nearby
Bus Tours: Yes

Morrisville

No Nonsense & More
1001 Airport Boulevard

Directions: Located right off I–40 at Raleigh Airport exit
Phone: (919) 380–7002
Hours: 10:00 A.M.–9:00 P.M., Monday–Saturday; 12:00–6:00 P.M., Sunday
Credit Cards: Discover, MasterCard, Visa
Personal Checks: Yes, with driver's license and one other form of identification
Food: Yes, food court
Bus Tours: Yes. Call center management for information.
Notes or Attractions: Located near Raleigh and the North Carolina Research Triangle Park

Nags Head

Soundings Factory Stores
U.S. Highway 158

Directions: U.S. Highway 158 at U.S. Highway 264, Mile Post 16½ on the By–Pass
Phone: (919) 441–7395
Hours: *January–March:* 10:00 A.M.–6:00 P.M., Monday–Saturday; 1:00–6:00 P.M., Sunday. *April–December:* 10:00 A.M.–9:00 P.M., Monday–Saturday; 1:00–6:00 P.M., Sunday.
Outlets:
Aileen
Arrow Factory Store
Bass Shoes
Benetton
Bugle Boy
Cabin Creek
Corning Revere
Fragrance Cove

Islandgear
Island Shirt
Jerzees
Jones New York
L'eggs/Hanes/Bali
London Fog
Pfaltzgraff
Publisher's Warehouse
Rack Room Shoes
Ruff Hewn
Socks Galore and More
Tie One On
Van Heusen
Wallet Works
Westport
Credit Cards: Varies from store to store
Personal Checks: Varies from store to store
Food: Yes, fast food
Bus Tours: Yes
Notes or Attractions: Located on an island. Surrounded by numerous tourist attractions.

Raleigh

Barry Manufacturing Company
6429–B Glenwood Avenue

Directions: Take the Glenwood Avenue exit off I–40
Phone: (919) 787–4493
Hours: 10:00 A.M.–9:00 P.M., Monday–Friday; 9:00 A.M.–6:00 P.M. Saturday; 12:00–5:00 P.M., Sunday
Credit Cards: American Express, Discover, MasterCard, Visa

Personal Checks: Yes
Food: Fast food nearby
Bus Tours: Yes
Notes or Attractions: Raleigh is the state capital and home to several colleges and universities.

Hamrick's of Raleigh
3529 Maitland Drive
Tower Shopping Complex

Directions: At U.S. Highway 64E and I–440 Beltline
Phone: (919) 231–8428
Hours: 10:00 A.M.–9:00 P.M., Monday–Saturday
Credit Cards: Discover, MasterCard, Visa
Personal Checks: Yes, with valid driver's license
Food: Available in immediate area
Bus Tours: Yes. Bus driver and one host receive $15 off total purchase with thirteen or more passengers. All bus passengers receive a free gift.

Rolane Factory Outlet
3511 Maitland Drive

Directions: From I–40, take I–440 East to Rocky Mount exit. Take U–turn at first intersection (Trawick Road) and right turn at Shoney's to enter center. Store is across from Red Roof Inn.
Phone: (919) 231–8394
Hours: 10:00 A.M.–9:00 P.M., Monday–Saturday; 1:00–6:00 P.M., Sunday
Credit Cards: Discover, MasterCard, Visa
Personal Checks: Yes, with driver's license
Food: Restaurants and cafeteria nearby
Alternate Transportation: Taxi, Raleigh public bus service, Raleigh miniline

Smithfield

Factory Stores of America
Industrial Park Drive

Directions: From I–95, take exit 95 (or 97); Industrial Park Drive and billboard signage will direct you to the outlet center, which is visible from I–95. From U.S. Highway 70 or 70 Business, turn onto Industrial Park Drive.
Phone: (919) 934–1157
Hours: 9:00 A.M.–9:00 P.M., Monday–Saturday; 1:00–6:00 P.M., Sunday. Call in advance for winter hours in January and February.
Outlets:
Aileen
American Tourister
Ann's Diamond Center
Banister Shoes
Bass Shoes
Benetton
Best Buys
Bikini World
Bon Worth
Book Warehouse
Boot Factory
Bugle Boy
Capezio
Carolina Clock & Rug
Carolina Linens
Carolina Pottery
Casual Male Big & Tall
Duck Head
Hathaway Shirt
Leather Loft
Le Creuset

L'eggs/Hanes/Bali
Levi's
London Fog
Nike
$9.99 Stockroom
Olga/Warner's
Paper Factory
Prestige Fragrance & Cosmetics, PFC Fragrance
Ribbon Outlet
Royal Doulton
S & K Menswear
Socks Galore and More
Totes/Sunglass World
Toy Liquidators
Van Heusen
Westport

Credit Cards: MasterCard and Visa accepted at all outlets throughout the center; American Express accepted at almost half the stores

Personal Checks: Yes, at all stores

Food: Food court on premises features two restaurants with such specialties as barbecued pork, fried chicken, yogurt, Italian food, and burgers.

Bus Tours: Yes. On-premises signage directs bus tours to Carolina Pottery's customer service area, where groups are welcomed and receive discount coupon booklets. The escort and driver receive gift certificates.

Notes or Attractions: The center is just minutes away from Southland Estate Winery, the Ava Gardner Museum, and the Tobacco Museum of North Carolina. The Smithfield–Selma Area Visitors Center is adjacent to the Carolina Pottery Outlet Center. A movie theater, three public golf courses, and a public swimming pool are within the immediate area. The outlet center is situated in an area that's perfect for walking or jogging. Future plans include a miniature golf course and batting cages.

Wilmington

Hamrick's of Wilmington
University Centre
356 S. College Road

Directions: Take Highway 74 into Wilmington until you see a sign for UNC–Wilmington. Take a right onto College Road. Hamrick's is 5 miles down on the left.
Phone: (919) 395–1491
Hours: 10:00 A.M.–9:00 P.M., Monday–Saturday
Credit Cards: Discover, MasterCard, Visa
Personal Checks: Yes, with valid driver's license
Food: Available in the immediate area
Bus Tours: Yes. Bus driver and one host receive $15 off total purchase with thirteen or more passengers. All bus passengers receive a free gift.

Rolane Factory Outlet
Outlet Mall
808 S. College Road

Directions: I–40 becomes College Road (Highway 132). Store is 3 miles on right.
Phone: (919) 791–8644
Hours: 10:00 A.M.–8:00 P.M., Monday–Saturday; 1:00–6:00 P.M., Sunday
Credit Cards: Discover, MasterCard, Visa
Personal Checks: Yes, with driver's license
Food: Restaurant in center of mall
Notes or Attractions: Seven miles from famous North Carolina beaches

Winston-Salem

Barry Manufacturing Company
1445 Trademart Boulevard

Directions: Take I–40 to Trademark Exit.
Phone: (919) 785–9810
Hours: 9:00 A.M.–6:00 P.M., Monday–Saturday (until 9:00 P.M. Friday);
12:00–5:00 P.M., Sunday
Credit Cards: American Express, Discover, MasterCard, Visa
Personal Checks: Yes
Food: Fast food nearby
Bus Tours: Yes

Hamrick's of Winston-Salem
Parkway Plaza
1253 Corporation Parkway

Directions: Take I–85 to I–77 toward Statesville. Take exit 38, then I–40E toward Winston-Salem to exit 51A. Take a right off exit and 2 miles down take a left onto Silas Creek Parkway. Take a left at first light into Hamrick's parking lot.
Phone: (919) 725–0390
Hours: 9:00 A.M.–8:00 P.M., Monday–Saturday
Credit Cards: Discover, MasterCard, Visa
Personal Checks: Yes, with valid driver's license
Food: Available in the immediate area
Bus Tours: Yes. Bus driver and one host will receive $15 off total purchase with thirteen or more passengers. Each bus passenger will receive a free gift.

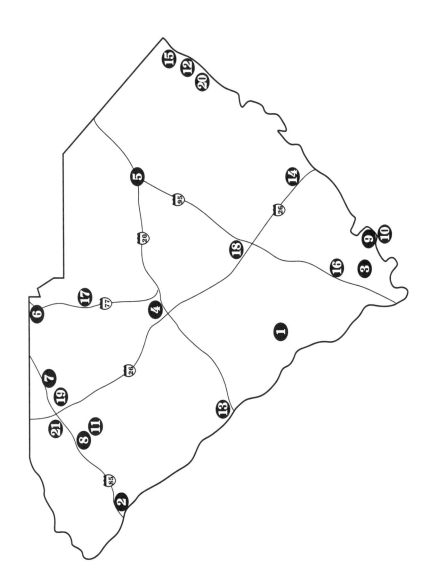

South Carolina

Numbers at the left of this legend correspond to the numbers on the accompanying map. The number to the right of each city's or town's name is the page number on which that municipality's outlets first appear in this book.

Allendale

Rolane Factory Outlet
301 North Main Street

Phone: (803) 584–4571
Credit Cards: Discover, MasterCard, Visa
Personal Checks: Yes, with driver's license

Anderson

Hamrick's of Anderson
Belvedere Plaza
3100 N. Main Street

Directions: Take I–85 to exit 19A. Hamrick's is 3 miles down on the left.
Phone: (803) 225–6637
Hours: 9:00 A.M.–9:00 P.M., Monday–Saturday
Credit Cards: Discover, MasterCard, Visa
Personal Checks: Yes, with valid driver's license
Food: Available in the immediate area
Bus Tours: Yes. Bus driver and one host receive $15 off total purchase with thirteen or more passengers. All bus passengers receive a free gift.

Bluffton

Low Country Factory Outlet Village
1024 Highway 278

Directions: Located on Highway 278 at the gateway to Hilton Head.
Phone: (803) 837–4339
Hours: *January–February:* 10:00 A.M.–7:00 P.M., Monday–Saturday; 12:00–6:00 P.M., Sunday. *March–December:* 10:00 A.M.–9:00 P.M., Monday–Saturday; 12:00–6:00 P.M., Sunday.

Outlets:
American Tourister
Baby Guess
Bass Shoes
Book Warehouse
Bugle Boy
Cape Isle Knitters
Capezio
Career Image
Corning Revere
Damon/Enro
Dan River
Danskin
Eddie Bauer
Famous Brands Housewares
Famous Footwear
Galt Sand
Geoffrey Beene
Gitano
Gold Toe
Goodwin Weavers
Islandgear
Island Shirt
J. Crew
Kitchen Collection
Levi's
London Fog
Maidenform
Micki Designer Separates
NCS Shoe
Olga/Warner's
Oneida
Prestige Fragrance & Cosmetics, PFC Fragrance
Reebok
Ribbon Outlet
Toy Liquidators
Trader Kids
Van Heusen

Westport
Windsor Shirt
Young Generations
Credit Cards: American Express, Discover, MasterCard, Visa
Personal Checks: Yes, but varies by store; mainly with driver's license and major credit card
Food: Food court on premises
Bus Tours: Yes. Motorcoach parking behind Galt Sand. Free coupon books valued at more than $45 and a shopping bag to each passenger. Free meal to the drivers and tour guides. Check in at Galt Sand or call the mall office for a free, personalized welcome.
Notes or Attractions: Beach plus nationally acclaimed golf and tennis facilities ten minutes away; historic Beaufort, South Carolina, and Savannah, Georgia, thirty minutes away

Columbia

Barry Manufacturing Company
6525 Two Notch Road

Directions: Two Notch Road is right off I–20 near Columbia Mall.
Phone: Main office, (404) 451–5476
Hours: 10:00 A.M.–7:00 P.M., Monday–Thursday; 10:00 A.M.–9:00 P.M., Friday; 9:00 A.M.–6:00 P.M., Saturday; 1:00–5:00 P.M., Sunday
Credit Cards: American Express, Discover, MasterCard, Visa
Personal Checks: Yes
Food: Fast food
Bus Tours: Yes
Notes or Attractions: Near the University of South Carolina

Hamrick's of Columbia
Outlet Pointe
300 Outlet Pointe Boulevard

Directions: Take I–20 to Bush River Road, exit 63. At second light, turn left. Hamrick's is straight ahead.
Phone: (803) 772–1060

Hours: 10:00 A.M.–9:00 P.M., Monday–Saturday
Credit Cards: Discover, MasterCard, Visa
Personal Checks: Yes, with valid driver's license
Food: Available in and around Outlet Pointe
Bus Tours: Yes. Bus driver and one host will receive $15 off total purchase with thirteen or more passengers. Each bus passenger will receive a free gift.

U.S. Textile Outlet
3130 Bluff Road

Directions: Approximately 3 miles past the University of South Carolina stadium on the left in the Columbia Industrial Park
Hours: 9:00 A.M.–4:00 P.M., Monday–Saturday
Credit Cards: MasterCard, Visa
Personal Checks: Yes
Food: Nearby
Bus Tours: Yes
Notes or Attractions: This outlet is attached to the factory, so the customer receives the lowest possible prices.

Florence

Hamrick's of Florence
Crossroads Center
2600 David McLeod Boulevard

Directions: Take I–20 into Florence; at first stoplight take a right, then an immediate left. Hamrick's is on the right.
Phone: (803) 669–7444
Hours: 9:00 A.M.–9:00 P.M., Monday–Saturday
Credit Cards: Discover, MasterCard, Visa
Personal Checks: Yes, with valid driver's license
Food: Available in the immediate area
Bus Tours: Yes. Bus driver and one host receive $15 off total purchase with thirteen or more passengers. All bus passengers receive a free gift.

Fort Mill

Outlet Marketplace
3700 Avenue of the Carolinas

Directions: Take I–77 south of Charlotte, North Carolina; or I–77 north of Columbia, South Carolina, exit 90 at Carowinds Boulevard
Phone: (803) 548–5888
Hours: 10:00 A.M.–9:00 P.M., Monday–Saturday; 1:30–6:00 P.M., Sunday; closed Thanksgiving Day and Christmas Day
Outlets:
Aileen
Banister Shoes
Bass Shoes
Belgian Rug Company
Cape Isle Knitters
Carolina Pottery
Corning Revere
County Seat
Designer Sunglasses
Famous Footwear
Forever Yours
Hamrick's
Love's Diamond and Jewelry
Prestige Fragrance & Cosmetics, PFC Fragrance
Publisher's Warehouse
Ribbon Outlet
Rolane Factory Outlet
Springmaid/Wamsutta
Van Heusen
Wallet Works
Westport
Credit Cards: Varies from store to store
Personal Checks: Varies from store to store
ATM: Yes
Food: A variety of fast food, ice cream, and confections
Bus Tours: Yes. Parking on side of mall for larger vehicles. Coupon books available in mall office.

Notes or Attractions: Located directly across from Carowinds Theme Park and close to the New Heritage USA. Approximately 10 miles from beautiful Charlotte, North Carolina.

Gaffney

Hamrick's of Cherokee Avenue
2508 Cherokee Avenue

Directions: Take I–85 to exit 90 and turn onto Highway 105 toward Gaffney. At first stoplight take a left onto Highway 29. Stay on Highway 29 through the town of Gaffney. Hamrick's is on your right.
Phone: (803) 487–6096
Hours: 9:00 A.M.–5:00 P.M., Monday–Saturday
Personal Checks: Yes, with valid driver's license
Bus Tours: Yes
Notes or Attractions: Unlike the regular Hamrick's description, this location only handles irregulars, closeouts, samples, and first-quality apparel and shoes.

Hamrick's
742 Peachoid Road

Directions: I–85 to exit at Highway 105
Phone: (803) 489–6095
Hours: 9:00 A.M.–7:00 P.M., Monday–Saturday
Credit Cards: Discover, MasterCard, Visa
Personal Checks: Yes, with major credit card and driver's license
Additional Savings: Clearance sale in January/February and July/August. In October, during Octoberfest, there are several in-store promotions.
Food: Yes, a cafeteria
Bus Tours: Yes. Bus driver and host get a free lunch and $15 coupon off one purchase with twelve or more people. All visitors arriving on a bus receive a free gift. All this is done at the front of the store.
Notes or Attractions: See the Peach Water Tower

Greenville

Hamrick's of Greenville
Westgate Plaza Shopping Center
7916 White Horse Road

Directions: Take I–85 to exit 44 onto White Horse Road, and take a right off exit. Follow several miles until you see Hamrick's on the left.
Phone: (803) 246–0822
Hours: 9:00 A.M.–9:00 P.M., Monday–Saturday
Credit Cards: Discover, MasterCard, Visa
Personal Checks: Yes, with valid driver's license
Bus Tours: Yes. Bus driver and one host receive $15 off total purchase with thirteen or more passengers. Each bus passenger receives a free gift.

HomeMaker Bedspread Outlet
Westgate Plaza Shopping Center
7912 White Horse Road

Directions: Take exit 44 off I–85. Go north on Highway 25 for approximately 8 miles.
Phone: (803) 246–3600
Hours: 9:30 A.M.–6:00 P.M., Monday–Saturday; closed Sunday
Credit Cards: MasterCard, Visa
Personal Checks: Yes, but must provide a valid driver's license, street address (or nearest road), and phone number
Additional Savings: Sales are offered around major holidays: Memorial Day, July 4th, Labor Day, Thanksgiving, and Christmas
Food: Yes, 2 blocks away
Bus Tours: Yes, with plenty of parking
Alternate Transportation: City bus stop at front door of store
Notes or Attractions: Located on a scenic highway to the mountains of North Carolina. Also near Furman University and Bob Jones University. Within the immediate area, there are parks, a golf course, boating, theaters, and a zoo. Ask for information on outdoor concerts.

Ribbon Outlet
North Rivers Market

Directions: From I–26, turn left onto Ashley Phosphate Road. Take another left onto Rivers Avenue. The outlet is approximately 1 mile on the right.
Phone: (803) 271–3894
Credit Cards: MasterCard, Visa
Personal Checks: Yes, with proper identification
Food: Nearby

West Point Pepperell Bed, Bath and Linens Factory Outlet
2712 Laurens Road

Directions: Take exit 48B off I–85 at Greenville and go north toward Greenville; the store is located a quarter mile on the left.
Phone: (803) 288–7752
Hours: 9:00 A.M.–6:00 P.M., Monday–Saturday (until 8:00 P.M. Friday); 1:30–6:00 P.M., Sunday
Credit Cards: MasterCard, Visa
Personal Checks: Yes, with proper identification; $100 limit on out-of-state checks
ATM: Nearby at Nations Bank
Food: Restaurants and fast-food establishments in the immediate area
Bus Tours: Yes
Notes or Attractions: Greenville is an important textile center. Very close by is the Waccamaw Pottery outlet in Spartanburg.

Hilton Head

Shoppes on the Parkway
Highway 278 (William Hilton Parkway)

Directions: Located on Highway 278 (William Hilton Parkway) between Palmetto Dunes and the shipyard
Phone: Corporate leasing offices, (615) 373–5427

Hours: *January–February:* 10:00 A.M.–6:00 P.M., Monday–Saturday; 1:00–6:00 P.M., Sunday. *March–December:* 10:00 A.M.–9:00 P.M., Monday–Saturday; 1:00–6:00 P.M., Sunday.

Outlets:
Aileen
Anne Klein
Carole Little
Dansk
Duck Head
Euro Collections/Bleyle
First Choice
Gilligan & O'Malley
Gorham
harvé benard
Hilton Head Shirt
Island Wear/Swimsuit Source
Jonathan Logan
Jones New York
Leather Loft
L'eggs/Hanes/Bali
Palmetto Textile/Linen Outlet
Paul Revere Shoppe
Player's World of Golf
Prestige Fragrance & Cosmetics, PFC Fragrance
Rack Room Shoes
Royal Robbins
Shoe Strings
Silkworm
Tie One On
Totes/Sunglass World
Van Heusen

Credit Cards: Discover, MasterCard, Visa
Personal Checks: Varies from store to store
Food: Fast-food establishments within the mall
Bus Tours: Yes
Notes or Attractions: Located within a coastal tourist area that offers golfing, tennis, and beaches. Other factory outlets are close by.

Hilton Head Island

Pineland Mill Shops
403 William Hilton Parkway

Directions: Pineland Mill Shops are located on Highway 278 (William Hilton Parkway), the only road on and off Hilton Head Island, at the intersection of Mathews Drive
Phone: (803) 681–8907
Hours: *March 1 to December 24:* 9:00 A.M.–8:00 P.M., Monday–Saturday; 12:00–5:00 P.M., Sunday. *December 26 to February 28:* 10:00 A.M.–6:00 P.M., Monday–Saturday; 12:00–5:00 P.M., Sunday.
Outlets:
Adolfo II
Barbizon Lingerie
Bass Shoes
Black & Decker
Cape Isle Knitters
designer's extras
Famous Footwear
Fieldcrest/Cannon
Heritage Fine Jewelry
Hilton Head Shirt
I.B. Diffusion
International Silver
Patchington
Polly Flinders
Royal Doulton
S & K Menswear
Shoe Strings
Swank
Tanner
Credit Cards: Varies by store; generally, American Express, Discover, MasterCard, Visa
Personal Checks: Yes. Most stores require a valid driver's license and a major credit card.
ATM: Yes, several in the immediate area
Additional Savings: Sidewalk sales in mid-August and Memorial Day

weekend. Tent sales are also held periodically throughout the summer. Moonlight Madness Sale in October.

Food: Yes, a large variety

Bus Tours: Yes. Discount coupons and free lunches for drivers and organizers are available if requested in advance.

Notes or Attractions: Pineland Mill Shops is located on South Carolina's largest barrier island at the southernmost edge of the state and attracts a large visitor and convention population. Hilton Head Island's natural beauty can be enjoyed year-round because it is positioned southerly enough to escape the harsh blast of winter. Hilton Head Island boasts some of the best recreational facilities in the world. Besides the 12 miles of sugar-sand beach, visitors can also enjoy exciting golf on fifteen public courses, great tennis at one of the seven racquet clubs, plus fishing, cycling, horseback riding, croquet, and entertainment and activities geared to a variety of audiences.

Mauldin

Just Kids
400 Bon Air Street

Directions: Approximately 3 miles off I–85. Take Highway 276 through Mauldin and bear left on Highway 417 over the bridge.

Phone: (803) 288–2642

Hours: 10:00 A.M.–6:00 P.M., Monday–Saturday

Credit Cards: Discover, MasterCard, Visa

Personal Checks: Yes

Food: Yes, nearby

Bus Tours: Yes

Myrtle Beach

Dansk Factory Outlet
3146 Waccamaw Boulevard

Directions: From North Myrtle Beach or the Myrtle Beach Airport, take U.S. Highway 17 Bypass to U.S. Highway 501, Conway exit. Go west, cross bridge. Outlet is on the right across the highway from Waccamaw Pottery.
Phone: (803) 236–1144
Hours: *June–August:* 9:30 A.M.–7:00 P.M., Monday–Saturday; 10:00 A.M.–6:00 P.M., Sunday. *September–May:* 10:00 A.M.–6:00 P.M., Monday–Sunday.
Credit Cards: MasterCard, Visa
Personal Checks: Yes
Food: A variety in the immediate area
Bus Tours: Yes

Hamrick's of Myrtle Beach
Village Square Shopping Center
4103 North King's Highway

Directions: Located on Highway 17-Business
Phone: (803) 448–5290
Hours: 10:00 A.M.–9:00 P.M., Monday–Saturday
Credit Cards: Discover, MasterCard, Visa
Personal Checks: Yes, with valid driver's license
Food: Available in the immediate area
Bus Tours: Yes. Bus driver and one host receive $15 off total purchase with thirteen or more passengers. All bus passengers receive a free gift.

Outlet Park at Waccamaw
U.S. Highway 501 at the Intracoastal Waterway

Directions: Take Highway 501 to the Intracoastal Waterway (2½ miles west of Myrtle Beach). Highway signage directs customers into Outlet Park. Park is clearly visible from the highway.

Phone: (803) 236–4606; Visitor Center (803) 236–6152; out of state (800) 444–VALU
Hours: *Winter:* 9:00 A.M.–6:00 P.M., Monday–Sunday. *Spring:* 9:00 A.M.–9:00 P.M., Monday–Saturday; 9:00 A.M.–6:00 P.M., Sunday. *Summer:* 9:00 A.M.–10:00 P.M., Monday–Saturday; 9:00 A.M.–6:00 P.M., Sunday. *Fall:* 9:00 A.M.–9:00 P.M., Monday–Saturday; 9:00 A.M.–6:00 P.M., Sunday.
Outlets:

Mall 1
American Eagle Outfitters
Bon Worth
Damon/Enro
Dollar Tree
Duck Head
Easy Spirit & Co.
Fancy Free Kids
Formfit
Jewelry Kingdom
Jody's Accessories
Jonathan Logan
Leslie Fay
London Fog
Manhattan
Newport
Oneita
SBX
Shoe Store for Less
Stanly Knitting Mill
Swank
Tanner
Toy Outlet
United Apparel, Ltd.

Mall 2
Accessory Stop
Adolfo II
Bagmakers
Barbizon Lingerie
Bath Stop

Bike Athletic
Boot Factory
Burlington Brands
Career Image
Carolina Clock & Rug
Casual Male Big & Tall
Children's Outlet
Dress Barn
Dress Barn Woman
Ducks Unlimited
Foot Factory
Fruit of the Loom
Gold Outlet
Hush Puppies
Jaymar
Magnavox
Naturalizer, Etc.
Oneida
Reader's Outlet
Sox Shoppe
Sunshades 501, Ltd.
Top of the Line Fragrances and
    Cosmetics
Trader Kids
United Apparel, Ltd.
Wallet Works

Mall 3
Aileen
American Tourister
Anne Klein

Arrow Factory Store
Audrey Jones
B&G Leather Hut
Bass Shoes
Book Warehouse
Boston Traders
Bugle Boy
Cape Isle Knitters
Capezio
Champion-Hanes
Eddie Bauer
Eyewear House
Famous Footwear
Fashion Flair
Fieldcrest/Cannon
Gals Direct
Generra Sportswear
Geoffrey Beene
Gift Depot
Gold & Silver Connection
Hit or Miss
Jaymar
J. Crew
Jones New York
Land & Sea Leather

Laura Ashley
L'eggs/Hanes/Bali
Leslie Fay
L.J.'s Fashions
Music 4 Less
Nautical Nook
OshKosh B'Gosh (The Genuine Article)
Polly Flinders
Prestige Fragrance & Cosmetics, PFC Fragrance
Rack Room Shoes
Ribbon Outlet
S & K Menswear
Shoe Show
Socks Galore and More
South Carolina Sportswear
Sports Wearhouse
Swank
Tie One On
Totes/Sunglass World
Toy Liquidators
Van Heusen
Young Generations

Credit Cards: Varies by store; generally, American Express, Discover, MasterCard, Visa

Personal Checks: Yes. Two forms of identification are necessary—a valid driver's license and a major credit card.

Additional Savings: Back-to-school sales in mid-August, summer clearance sales, after-Christmas sales; special coupons to tour groups

Food: Food court located in Mall 2; food service located in Mall 3; four area restaurants conveniently available

Alternate Transportation: Bus service to Outlet Park by CRPTA

Bus Tours: Yes. A visitor's center is located on the premises, (803) 236–6152. Drivers and coordinators receive lunch coupons and $10 gift certificate.

Notes or Attractions: The Outlet Park shopping area is served by a forty-seat passenger tram that transports shoppers throughout the three-mall complex. Sites of interest in the area: the Carolina Opry; the Dixie Jubilee; the Dixie Stampede; Southern Country Nights; Great Country Legends; the Alabama Theatre; Wild Water and Wheels; the Myrtle Beach Pavilion; Brookgreen Gardens; Myrtle Waves Water Park; movie theaters on the premises; 3 miles from the Atlantic Ocean; 75 golf courses in the area.

North Augusta

Hamrick's of North Augusta
North Augusta Plaza
320 E. Martintown Road

Directions: Take I–20 toward Columbia. Take exit 4 for North Augusta. Follow Martintown Road to Hamrick's on the right.
Phone: (803) 279–4212
Hours: 9:00 A.M.–7:00 P.M., Monday–Saturday
Credit Cards: Discover, MasterCard, Visa
Personal Checks: Yes, with valid driver's license
Food: Available in the immediate area
Bus Tours: Yes. Bus driver and one host receive $15 off total purchase with thirteen or more passengers. All bus passengers receive a free gift.

North Charleston

Barry Manufacturing Company
5624 Rivers Avenue

Phone: (803) 554–5318
Hours: 10:00 A.M.–7:00 P.M., Monday–Thursday; 10:00 A.M.–9:00 P.M., Friday; 9:00 A.M.–6:00 P.M., Saturday; 1:00–5:00 P.M., Sunday
Credit Cards: American Express, Discover, MasterCard, Visa
Personal Checks: Yes
Food: Nearby

Bus Tours: Yes
Notes or Attractions: Within an easy drive of all the excitement and history of Charleston

Hamrick's of North Charleston
Festival Centre
5101 Ashley Phosphate Road

Directions: Take I–26 to exit 209 onto Ashley Phosphate Road. Hamrick's is at the corner of Ashley Phosphate and Dorchester Road.
Phone: (803) 760–2211
Hours: 9:00 A.M.–8:00 P.M., Monday–Saturday
Credit Cards: Discover, MasterCard, Visa
Personal Checks: Yes, with driver's license
Food: Available in the area
Bus Tours: Yes. Bus driver and one host receive $15 off total purchase with thirteen or more passengers. All bus passengers receive a free gift.

North Myrtle Beach

Barefoot Landing
Highway 17

Directions: Arrive by boat from the Intracoastal Waterway or take Highway 17 from North Myrtle Beach, south, or Myrtle Beach, north.
Phone: (803) 272–8349; (800) 272–2320
Hours: 10:00 A.M.–11:00 P.M., Monday–Sunday. (Varies by season. Call ahead.)
Outlets:
Bass Shoes
Cape Isle Knitters
Capezio
Covers 'N Stuff
Geoffrey Beene
Gilligan & O'Malley
Handbag Company

London Fog
Outerbanks
Rack Room Shoes
S & K Menswear
Van Heusen
Westport
Credit Cards: Varies by outlet
Personal Checks: Varies by outlet
Food: Waterfront dining at a large variety of establishments
Bus Tours: Yes
Notes or Attractions: Attractively laid out, this complex offers outlet and regular retail shopping. Located right at the beach. Received the 1991 Most Outstanding Attraction award from the South Carolina Chamber of Commerce.

Point South

Sabatier Cutlery
Highway 17 North and I–95, exit 33
(Mailing address: P.O. Box 574, Yemassee, SC 29945)

Directions: As noted in the above address
Phone: (803) 726–6444; (800) 525–6399; Fax (803) 726–6713
Hours: 8:00 A.M.–6:00 P.M., Monday–Sunday
Credit Cards: American Express, Discover, MasterCard, Visa
Personal Checks: Yes, with valid driver's license
Food: Restaurants within walking distance
Bus Tours: Yes
Notes or Attractions: Campground nearby

Richburg

The Interior Alternative
Frederic Drive

Directions: From I–77, take exit 65, Route 9. Go north on Route 9 approximately six-tenths of a mile to Lyles Road. Turn right. Take next right onto Frederic Drive. Follow signs to rear of building to store entrance.
Phone: (803) 789–6655
Hours: 10:00 A.M.–5:00 P.M., Monday–Saturday. Closed most corporate holidays and one week between Christmas and New Year's Day.
Credit Cards: MasterCard, Visa
Personal Checks: North and South Carolina only, with valid driver's license
Food: McDonalds, Kentucky Fried Chicken, Waffle House, Country Omelet, The Front Porch restaurant all located at Route 9 exit
Bus Tours: Yes, but call ahead so that the staff will be prepared. Group discounts can be arranged.
Notes or Attractions: Located halfway between Charlotte, North Carolina, and Columbia, South Carolina, on I–77.

Santee

Santee Factory Stores
I–95 at exit 98

Directions: Take I–95 to exit 98 (which is Highway 6)
Phone: (803) 854–4445
Hours: 9:00 A.M.–8:00 P.M., Monday–Saturday; 1:30 P.M.–6:00 P.M., Sunday
Outlets:
Aileen
Banister Shoes
Bass Shoes
Bikini World
Bon Worth
Book Warehouse

Brass Factory
Bugle Boy
Duck Head
Famous Footwear
Farberware, Inc.
Fashion Flair
Fieldcrest/Cannon
Florsheim Shoe
Kitchen Collection
L'eggs/Hanes/Bali
London Fog
Napier
Oneida
Paper Factory
Prestige Fragrance & Cosmetics, PFC Fragrance
Royal Doulton
Swank
Totes/Sunglass World
Van Heusen
Westport
Credit Cards: Varies by outlet, but most major cards accepted
Personal Checks: Varies by outlet, but most with proper identification
Food: Yes, on-site
Bus Tours: Yes, preplan by calling (803) 854–4445.
Notes or Attractions: Located within minutes of Lake Marion

Spartanburg

Foothills Factory Stores
Interstate 26 at Interstate 85

Directions: I–26 at New Cut Road (exit 17). The park is clearly visible from I–26.
Phone: Foothills Factory Stores (803) 574–8587; WCI Management Office (803) 236–4606. Management Office is located at Foothills Factory Stores.

Hours: 10:00 A.M.–9:00 P.M., Monday–Saturday; 1:30–6:30 P.M., Sunday
Outlets:
Aileen
Arrow Factory Store
Bass Shoes
Bon Worth
Book Warehouse
Bugle Boy
Burlington Shoe
Dress Barn
Ducks Unlimited
Foot Factory
Gals Direct
Hit or Miss
L'eggs/Hanes/Bali
Levi's
Little Red Shoe House
Music 4 Less
Newport
Nina's Accessory World
One $ Store
One Price Clothing
Prestige Fragrance & Cosmetics, PFC Fragrance
Ribbon Outlet
Sunshades 501, Ltd.
Toy Liquidators
Van Heusen
Waccamaw Pottery
Credit Cards: Varies by store; generally American Express, Discover, MasterCard, Visa
Personal Checks: Yes. Two forms of identification are necessary—a valid driver's license and a major credit card.
Additional Savings: Back-to-school sales, clearance sales, after-Christmas sales
Food: Fast food available at the complex and nearby area
Bus Tours: Yes. A visitor's center is on the premises.
Alternate Transportation: Bus service available to complex from downtown Spartanburg

Reeves Discount Outlet
Highway 29 West

Directions: From I–85, take exit 66 east; the outlet is 2.1 miles farther on Highway 29 toward Spartanburg. From I–26, take exit 21A west; the outlet is 2.1 miles farther on Highway 29 toward Greer.
Phone: (803) 576–9252
Hours: 9:00 A.M.–5:00 P.M., Monday–Friday; 8:00 A.M.–4:00 P.M., Saturday
Credit Cards: MasterCard, Visa
Personal Checks: Yes
Food: No
Bus Tours: Yes. Free gift for driver and host. Extra 20 percent discount for group.

Surfside Beach

Owl-o-Rest
410–A Highway 17 North

Directions: Approximately 1 mile south of Highway 544 and Highway 17 Business intersection. Outlet is on the right, three doors south of Surfside Beach Post Office.
Phone: (803) 238–1902
Hours: 9:00 A.M.–6:00 P.M., Monday–Saturday
Credit Cards: American Express, Discover, MasterCard, Visa
Personal Checks: Yes
ATM: Yes
Food: Various fast-food establishments in the immediate vicinity
Bus Tours: Yes
Notes or Attractions: A coastal tourist area offering beaches, bowling, Brookgreen Gardens, and fresh seafood dining

Wellford

Famous Name Brand Shoes
181 Cannon Road

Directions: Located on Highway 29, 6 miles west of Spartanburg. Take exit 66 off I–85; then go south 1.5 miles. The store is on the left.
Phone: (803) 439–3557
Hours: 9:00 A.M.–6:00 P.M., Monday–Saturday
Credit Cards: Discover, MasterCard, Visa
Personal Checks: Yes
Food: Yes, all along the interstate (within 1 mile)
Bus Tours: Yes
Notes or Attractions: Other outlets are located off I–85 at exit 66.

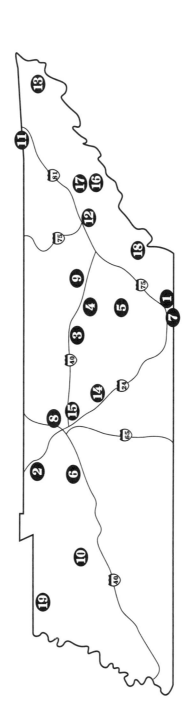

Tennessee

Numbers at the left of this legend correspond to the numbers on the accompanying map. The number to the right of each city's or town's name is the page number on which that municipality's outlets first appear in this book.

Chattanooga

Hamrick's of Chattanooga
Hamilton Village
2020 Gunbarrel Road

Directions: Take I–75 to exit 5 onto Shallowford Road. Turn right on Gunbarrel Road. Hamrick's is on the left.
Phone: (615) 499–5011
Hours: 10:00 A.M.–9:00 P.M., Monday–Saturday
Credit Cards: Discover, MasterCard, Visa
Personal Checks: Yes, with valid driver's license
Food: Available in the immediate area
Bus Tours: Yes. Bus driver and one host receive $15 off total purchase with thirteen or more passengers. All bus passengers receive a free gift.

Warehouse Row Factory Shops
1110 Market Street

Directions: From Knoxville: Take I–75 south to Chattanooga to the I–24 split. Veer right at split to I–24 west. Take exit 178 to North Market Street. Proceed to fifth traffic signal at Houston Street.
Phone: (615) 267–1111
Hours: 10:00 A.M.–7:00 P.M., Monday–Saturday; 12:00–6:00 P.M., Sunday. Extended hours Memorial Day–Labor Day: 10:00 A.M.–8:00 P.M., Monday–Saturday; 12:00–7:00 P.M., Sunday. (Call to confirm holiday hours.)
Outlets:
Adrienne Vittadini
Bass Shoes
Cape Isle Knitters
Carroll Reed
Coach
Cole-Haan
Colours
Corbin
designer's extras

Ellen Tracy
First Choice
Fragrance Cove
Geoffrey Beene
Goldsmith Shop
Guess?
HE-RO Group
I.B. Diffusion
J. Crew
Johnston & Murphy
Kelly Stryker
Napier
Nautica
Nickels
Perry Ellis
Polo/Ralph Lauren
President's Tailor
Ruff Hewn
Tanner
Van Heusen
Welcome Home
Westport

Credit Cards: Varies by store

Personal Checks: Varies by store

ATM: Branch bank located across from outlet center

Additional Savings: Mall-walk clearance sales at the end of summer and winter fashion seasons

Food: Food court on the premises featuring Italian, Chinese, French, and American cuisines

Bus Tours: Yes

Alternate Transportation: Reach Warehouse Row from downtown hotels and attractions via CARTA's free Downtown Shuttle.

Notes or Attractions: Chattanooga specializes in family vacations. Minutes from Warehouse Row is Lookout Mountain, where The Battle Above the Clouds was fought during the Civil War. Visit Point Park, Rock City, Ruby Falls, and ride the Incline Railway, all located on the mountain. Numerous Civil War parks in the area. The Tennessee Aquarium, the nation's first freshwater aquarium is less than ten minutes from Warehouse Row. Chattanooga Choo Choo located 2 blocks from the center. *Woman's Day* magazine has listed Warehouse Row as one of the top five outlet centers in the nation.

Clarksville

Acme Boot Outlet
3077 Guthrie Highway

Directions: From I–24, take exit 4, Highway 79 south. Outlet is about half a mile on the left between Shoney's and Best Western.
Phone: (615) 552–2000, ext. 267
Hours: 8:00 A.M.–9:00 P.M., Monday–Saturday; 10:00 A.M.–8:00 P.M., Sunday
Credit Cards: American Express, Discover, MasterCard, Visa
Personal Checks: Yes, with a valid driver's license or other identification
Food: Restaurants and fast-food establishments in the immediate area
Bus Tours: Yes; four hours' notice appreciated
Notes or Attractions: Theaters, arcades, and a museum are within a half-hour's drive. The area is dotted with antiques shops, historic sites, Austin Peavy State University, and Ft. Campbell Military Post. Outlet is five minutes away from Beachaven Winery.

Acme Boot Outlet
100 Providence Boulevard

Directions: From I–24, take exit 1, Highway 41A south. Outlet is approximately 7 miles on the right. From I–24, take exit 4, Highway 79 south. Turn right on Kraft Street, then right onto Highway 41A north. Outlet is on the left.
Hours: 9:00 A.M.–9:00 P.M., Monday–Saturday; 12:00–6:00 P.M., Sunday (open 10:00 A.M. between Thanksgiving and Christmas)
Credit Cards: American Express, Discover, MasterCard, Visa
Personal Checks: Yes, with valid driver's license or other identification
Food: Restaurants and fast-food establishments in the immediate area

Bus Tours: Yes
Notes or Attractions: Close to Land Between the Lakes. *Other Clarksville Locations:* 513 East Highway 131, (812) 282–7165 (take I–65 to exit 4); 2227 Madison Street, (615) 647–7949 (I–24, exit 11, inside the Acme Boot Company Distribution Center).

Cookeville

Acme Boot Outlet
803 South Jefferson

Directions: Located off I–40, between Nashville and Knoxville, exit 287. Turn left on S. Jefferson Avenue. Outlet is a quarter mile on the left across from a steak house.
Phone: (615) 552–2000, ext. 267
Hours: 8:00 A.M.–7:00 P.M., Monday, Tuesday, and Thursday; 8:00 A.M.–6:00 P.M., Wednesday; 8:00 A.M.–8:00 P.M., Friday–Saturday; 12:30–5:00 P.M., Sunday. Open Thanksgiving and Christmas; call for hours.
Credit Cards: American Express, Discover, MasterCard, Visa
Personal Checks: Yes, with valid driver's license or other identification
Food: Restaurants and fast-food establishments in the immediate area
Bus Tours: Yes
Notes or Attractions: Located in the hills of Tennessee. A bowling alley and miniature golf are within walking distance of the outlet.

Crossville

Aileen
Genesis Factory Outlet
211 Industrial Parkway

Directions: I–40, exit 321 to Industrial Parkway
Phone: (615) 456–7808
Hours: 9:00 A.M.–7:00 P.M., Monday–Thursday; 9:00 A.M.–8:00 P.M., Friday–Saturday; 11:00 A.M.–6:00 P.M., Sunday

Credit Cards: MasterCard, Visa
Personal Checks: Yes
Food: Barbecue and deli
Bus Tours: Yes. Ask about a coupon book.

VF Factory Outlet

Factory Stores of America Outlet Center
Genesis Road and I–40

Directions: From I–40 take exit 320, Genesis Road, go 1 block south, turn right, go 1 block. Outlet is located on the right.
Phone: (615) 484–7165
Hours: *January–May:* 9:00 A.M.–7:00 P.M., Monday–Thursday; 9:00 A.M.–8:00 P.M., Friday–Saturday; 12:00–5:30 P.M., Sunday. *June–October:* 9:00 A.M.–8:00 P.M., Monday–Thursday; 9:00 A.M.–9:00 P.M., Friday–Saturday; 12:00–5:30 P.M., Sunday. *November–December:* 9:00 A.M.–9:00 P.M., Monday–Saturday; 12:00–5:30 P.M., Sunday. Hours may change, so call ahead.
Credit Cards: Discover, MasterCard, Visa
Personal Checks: Yes, with proper identification
Food: Yes, nearby
Bus Tours: Yes. Free shopping bags and coupons for bus passengers. Free meal tickets for bus drivers and tour directors.
Notes or Attractions: Cumberland County Playhouse and Cumberland Mountain State Park are within 7 miles of the outlet. Fairfield Glade, Lake Tansi Village, and Thunder Hollow Resorts are within fifteen minutes. Knoxville, Nashville, Chattanooga, and the Great Smoky Mountains National Park are within two hours.

Dayton

Rolane Factory Outlet

159 East Main Street

Directions: From Highway 27 Bypass, come through Dayton. Turn onto West Main going toward downtown. Store is on the left.
Phone: (615) 775–3084

Hours: 10:00 A.M.–5:30 P.M., Monday–Thursday; 9:00 A.M.–6:00 P.M., Friday–Saturday; 1:00–5:30 P.M., Sunday
Credit Cards: Discover, MasterCard, Visa
Personal Checks: Yes, with driver's license
Food: Yes, in downtown Dayton, nearby
Notes or Attractions: Two blocks from the historic Dayton Courthouse, scene of the Scopes trial.

Dickson

Acme Boot Outlet
2327 Highway 46 South

Directions: Heading west on I–40, take exit 172, then bear right; the store is one block farther. Heading east on I–40, take exit 172 and turn right; the store is about 4 blocks on the right.
Phone: (615) 552–2000, ext. 267
Hours: 8:00 A.M.–9:00 P.M., Monday–Saturday; 10:00 A.M.–7:00 P.M., Sunday
Credit Cards: American Express, Discover, MasterCard, Visa
Personal Checks: Yes, with valid driver's license or other identification
Food: Steak houses and fast-food establishments nearby
Bus Tours: Yes; large parking lot in rear of store
Notes or Attractions: Montgomery Bell State Park is nearby. Within a half hour are Nashville and "Hurricane Mills," Loretta Lynn's dude ranch.

East Ridge

Acme Boot
East Ridge Antique Mall
6503 Slater Road

Directions: From I–75, take the East Ridge exit. Turn right. Outlet is half a mile on the right, behind Cracker Barrel.

Phone: (615) 552–2000, ext. 267
Hours: 9:00 A.M.–9:00 P.M., Monday–Saturday; 12:00–6:00 P.M., Sunday
Credit Cards: American Express, Discover, MasterCard, Visa
Personal Checks: Yes, with valid driver's license or other identification
Food: Restaurants and fast-food establishments in the immediate area
Bus Tours: Yes

Goodlettsville

Acme Boot Factory Outlet
Music City Outlet Mall
900 Conference Drive

Directions: From I–65 north, take exit 97. Outlet is behind Cracker Barrel as you turn right off exit.
Phone: (615) 851–1950
Hours: 9:00 A.M.–9:00 P.M., Monday–Saturday; 12:00–6:00 P.M., Sunday
Credit Cards: American Express, Discover, MasterCard, Visa
Personal Checks: Yes, with valid driver's license or other identification
Food: Yes, in the immediate area
Bus Tours: Yes
Notes or Attractions: Eight minutes north of downtown Nashville. Conway Twitty's home and Twitty City are fifteen minutes away.

Harriman

Acme Boot Factory Outlet
Highway 27 and 61

Directions: I–40, exit 347 and Highway 27 North. Outlet is about half a mile on the right.
Phone: (615) 882–6890
Hours: 9:00 A.M.–8:00 P.M., Monday–Saturday; 12:00–6:00 P.M., Sunday
Credit Cards: American Express, Discover, MasterCard, Visa

Personal Checks: Yes, with valid driver's license or other form of identification
Food: Yes, in vicinity
Bus Tours: Yes; advance notice appreciated
Notes or Attractions: Roane State Community College Exposition Center is six minutes away.

Humboldt

Dan's Factory Outlet
114 North Fourteenth Avenue

Directions: Exit I–40 at Highway 45 bypass north, in Jackson. Follow bypass to Humboldt downtown area. Turn right on Fourteenth Avenue.
Phone: (901) 784–3883
Hours: 9:00 A.M.–5:30 P.M., Monday–Friday; 9:00 A.M.–6:00 P.M., Saturday
Credit Cards: Discover, MasterCard, Visa
Personal Checks: Yes, with proper identification
ATM: Yes, nearby
Food: Fast food and restaurant within 1 mile
Bus Tours: Yes
Notes or Attractions: Beautiful countryside; a few minutes from Jackson

Kingsport

Burlington Coat Factory
1116 East Stone Drive

Directions: Take I–181 North from I–81, exit at Stone Drive. Turn right; store is approximately 3 miles on the left.
Phone: (615) 246–9751
Hours: 10:00 A.M.–9:30 P.M., Monday–Saturday; 12:00–6:00 P.M., Sunday. Closed Easter, Thanksgiving, and Christmas.
Credit Cards: American Express, Discover, MasterCard, Visa

Personal Checks: Yes
Food: Five restaurants within walking distance
Bus Tours: Yes
Notes or Attractions: This store is located in the tri-city area of eastern Tennessee, within one hour, or less, driving distance to North Carolina, Virginia, and Kentucky.

Hamrick's of Kingsport
Flagship Regional Center
1053 Flagship Drive

Directions: Take I–81 to exit 63, Airport Road
Phone: (615) 323–0340
Hours: 10:00 A.M.–9:00 P.M., Monday–Saturday
Credit Cards: Discover, MasterCard, Visa
Personal Checks: Yes, with valid driver's license
Food: Available in the immediate area
Bus Tours: Yes. Bus driver and one host receive $15 off total purchase with thirteen or more passengers. All bus passengers receive a free gift.

Knoxville

Acme Boot Factory Outlet
509 Lovell Road

Directions: From I–40, take the Lovell Road exit. Outlet is an eighth of a mile on the left.
Phone: (615) 552–2000, ext. 267
Hours: 9:00 A.M.–9:00 P.M., Monday–Saturday; 10:00 A.M.–6:00 P.M., Sunday
Credit Cards: American Express, Discover, MasterCard, Visa
Personal Checks: Yes, with valid driver's license or other form of identification
Food: Yes, in vicinity
Bus Tours: Yes; advance notice appreciated

Notes or Attractions: *Second location:* 5611 Merchants Center Boulevard (take I–75, exit 108, behind Red Lobster). Smoky Mountains are forty-five minutes away.

Hamrick's of Knoxville
Windsor Square
Kingston Pike

Directions: Take I–40 to exit 378. Take a left off the exit and stay in the right lane.
Phone: (615) 691–1013
Hours: 9:00 A.M.–8:00 P.M., Monday–Saturday
Credit Cards: Discover, MasterCard, Visa
Personal Checks: Yes, with valid driver's license
Food: Available in the area
Bus Tours: Yes. Bus driver and one host receive $15 off total purchase with thirteen or more passengers. All bus passengers receive a free gift.

Mountain City

Stanly Knitting Mill
Highway 421
Pioneer Village Shopping Center
150 South Shady Street

Directions: From Boone, North Carolina, take Highway 421 north to Mountain City. The outlet is located on the left behind Hardee's.
Phone: (615) 727–5323
Hours: 9:30 A.M.–5:30 P.M., Monday–Saturday
Credit Cards: Discover, MasterCard, Visa
Personal Checks: Yes, with two forms of identification
Food: Fast food and restaurants close by
Bus Tours: Yes, with plenty of parking
Notes or Attractions: Close to the mountains, with Boone and Blowing Rock approximately 24 miles away. A golf course is near the outlet.

Murfreesboro

Acme Boot Factory Outlet
1525 South Church Street

Directions: From I–24 west, take exit 81A for Murfreesboro. Outlet is approximately 1 mile on the right. From I–24 east, take Murfreesboro exit 81B. Outlet is approximately 1 mile on the right.
Phone: (615) 552–2000, ext. 267
Hours: 9:00 A.M.–9:00 P.M., Monday–Saturday; 12:00–6:00 P.M., Sunday
Credit Cards: American Express, Discover, MasterCard, Visa
Personal Checks: Yes, with valid driver's license
Food: Yes, in vicinity
Bus Tours: Yes; advance notice appreciated
Notes or Attractions: Miniature golf and other family activities in the area. Just twenty minutes away from Shelbyville, home of the Tennessee Walking Horse Celebration.

Outlets Ltd. Mall
Highway 96 West

Directions: I–24, exit 78, Highway 96 West
Phone: (615) 895–4966
Hours: 10:00 A.M.–9:00 P.M., Monday–Saturday; 1:00–6:00 P.M., Sunday
Outlets:
Acme Boot
Bass Shoes
Black & Decker
Book Island
Bruce Alan Bags
Bugle Boy
Casual Male Big & Tall
Donnkenny
Dress Barn
Dress Barn Woman
Duck Head
Electronic Express

Evan-Picone
Famous Footwear
Genesco Factory to You Store
Gold Rush
Hit or Miss
Hush Puppies
Izod
L'eggs/Hanes/Bali
Leslie Fay
Linens 'n Things
London Fog
Polly Flinders
Prestige Fragrance & Cosmetics, PFC Fragrance
Rack Room Shoes
SBX
Socks Galore and More
Sound Junction
Sunspecs Sunglass Superstore
Toy Liquidators
Treasure Chest
Van Heusen
Welcome Home
Credit Cards: Varies from store to store
Personal Checks: Varies from store to store
Food: Yes, fast food
Bus Tours: Yes

Nashville

Barry Manufacturing Company
2638 Nolansville Road

Directions: Nolansville Road is off I–65.
Phone: (615) 244–3350
Hours: 10:00 A.M.–8:00 P.M., Monday–Friday; 9:00 A.M.–6:00 P.M., Saturday; 12:00–5:00 P.M., Sunday

Credit Cards: American Express, Discover, MasterCard, Visa
Personal Checks: Yes
Food: Nearby
Bus Tours: Yes
Notes or Attractions: Near all the excitement of the Music City!

Pigeon Forge

Belz Factory Outlet Mall
2655 Teaster Lane

Directions: Enter Pigeon Forge from north or south on U.S. Highway 441 and follow directions on billboards.
Phone: (615) 453–7316
Hours: *January–March:* 10:00 A.M.–6:00 P.M., Sunday–Thursday; 10:00 A.M.–9:00 P.M., Friday–Saturday. *April–December:* 10:00 A.M.–9:00 P.M., Monday–Saturday; 10:00 A.M.–6:00 P.M., Sunday.
Outlets:

Accessories and Specialty Shops
Bag and Baggage
Book Factory
Coats and Clark
Crown Jewels
Diamond Factory & Eelskin
  Outlet
Everything's A Dollar
Fuller Brush
Jewelry Outlet
Knife Factory
Leather Loft
Music 4 Less
Old Time Pottery
Paper Factory
Prestige Fragrance & Cosmetics,
  PFC Fragrance
Ribbon Outlet

Seasons
Socks Galore and More
Toy Liquidators
Whims

Children's Wear
Gitano/Kids
Today's Child
Young Generations

Footwear
Bass Shoes
Boot Factory
Capezio
Converse Shoe
Etienne Aigner
Famous Footwear
General Shoe Factory to You

Hush Puppies
Nike
9 West
Rack Room Shoes

Housewares
Famous Brands Housewares
Regal Ware
Royal Doulton
West Point Pepperell Bed, Bath
    and Linens Factory Outlet

Men's, Women's, and Children's Wear
Amy Stoudt
Bike Athletic
Bon Worth
Bugle Boy
Burlington Brands
Casual Male Big & Tall
Champion-Hanes
Crazy Horse
Damon/Enro

designer's extras
Donnkenny
Dress Barn
Duck Head
Generra Sportswear
Gitano
Jockey
Jonathan Logan
Jordache
Judy Bond Blouses
Knits by K.T.
Levi's
Maidenform
$9.99 Stockroom
No Nonsense & More
Old Mill
Palm Beach
Petite Shop
Plumm's (E.J.)
Ruff Hewn
Ruthie's
Van Heusen
Westport

Due to corporate restrictions as outlined by this outlet mall, the publisher has been unable to provide profiles on the following outlets. These outlets have also been omitted from the indexes.

Fragrance Outlet
Jewelry & Leather Outlet
Just About Perfect
Lee Winter

Members Only
Shop at Home
Sports Extras
Sunglass Express

Credit Cards: Varies by store; generally, MasterCard, Visa
Personal Checks: Varies by store; generally yes, with the proper identification
Food: Two food courts in the mall

Bus Tours: Yes. Contact the mall office, (615) 453–7316.

Notes or Attractions: Located at the entrance of the Great Smoky Mountains, Belz Factory Outlet Mall in Pigeon Forge welcomed more than six million visitors in 1992. It is 5 miles from the resort area of Gatlinburg that remains a heavily visited tourist spot all year long. The center is in the heart of popular Pigeon Forge, where visitors will find numerous restaurants, motels, and shopping and entertainment opportunities.

Red Roof Outlet Mall/Factory Merchants Mall
Highway 441—On the Parkway

Directions: From Highway 411 east, take Highway 441 south. Where I–75 crosses I–40, take Highway 441 south to the Mall.

Phone: (615) 428–2828

Hours: *Season Hours:* 9:00 A.M.–9:00 P.M., Monday–Saturday; 9:00 A.M.–6:00 P.M., Sunday. *Off-season Hours:* 10:00 A.M.–6:00 P.M., Sunday–Thursday; 10:00 A.M.–9:00 P.M., Friday–Saturday.

Outlets:

Aileen
American Tourister
Arrow Factory Store
Aunt Mary's Yarns
Banister Shoes
Bass Shoes
Bike Athletic
Black & Decker
Bon Worth
Book Warehouse
Boston Traders
Carter's
Corning Revere
Evan-Picone
Fieldcrest/Cannon
Formfit
Full Size Fashions
Galt Sand

Geoffrey Beene
Gorham
Greetings 'N' More
Izod
Jaymar
Kitchen Collection
Langtry
L'eggs/Hanes/Bali
London Fog
Manhattan
Mikasa
No Nonsense & More
Oneida
OshKosh B'Gosh (The Genuine
    Article)
Perfumania
Pfaltzgraff
Polly Flinders

Sergio Valente
Socks Galore and More
Tanner
Top of the Line Fragrances and
    Cosmetics

Totes/Sunglass World
Van Heusen
Wallet Works

Due to corporate restrictions as outlined by this outlet mall, the publisher has been unable to provide profiles on the following outlets. These outlets also have been omitted from the indexes.

Banner House
Buxton
Chicago Cutlery
Morning Sun
Sergio Tacchini
Credit Cards: Varies by outlet
Personal Checks: Varies by outlet
Food: Yes, on-site
Bus Tours: Yes. Call to preplan, (615) 428–2828.
Notes or Attractions: Great Smoky Mountains twenty minutes away; Gatlinburg ten minutes away; Dollywood 5 miles away

Tanger Factory Outlet Center
175 Davis Road, Suite 14

Directions: From I–40, take Highway 407 exit and go to Pigeon Forge, approximately 12 miles from exit. Turn left at first traffic light (#3) in Pigeon Forge. First center is on the left.
Phone: (615) 428–7001; (800) 727–6885
Hours: *January–March:* 10:00 A.M.–6:00 P.M., Sunday–Thursday; 10:00 A.M.–9:00 P.M., Friday–Saturday. *April–December:* 9:00 A.M.–9:00 P.M., Monday–Saturday; 9:00 A.M.–6:00 P.M., Sunday.
Outlets:
Anne Klein
Barbizon Lingerie
Boston Trader Kids
Chaus
Coach

Dansk
Eddie Bauer
Farberware, Inc.
harvé benard
Izod
J. Crew
J. H. Collectibles
L'eggs/Hanes/Bali
Leslie Fay
Liz Claiborne
London Fog
Reebok
Samsonite
S & K Menswear
Springmaid/Wamsutta
Stone Mountain Handbags
Swank
WEMCO
Credit Cards: American Express, Discover, MasterCard, Visa
Personal Checks: Yes, with valid identification
ATM: One block away
Additional Savings: Spring and Summer Clearance (July and August); Fall and Winter Clearance (January and February)
Food: Deli Factory on the premises
Bus Tours: Yes; check in at mall office. Incentives for bus drivers and tour directors. Discount coupon.
Notes or Attractions: Vacation destination for Smoky Mountains National Park and Dollywood.

Sevierville

Aileen
Five Oaks Factory Stores
1645 Parkway, Suite 210

Directions: From I–40, take exit 407 onto Highway 441. Outlet is approximately 7 miles south on the left.

Phone: (615) 429–1640
Hours: 9:00 A.M.–9:00 P.M., Monday–Saturday; 9:00 A.M.–7:00 P.M., Sunday
Credit Cards: MasterCard, Visa
Personal Checks: Yes
Food: Restaurant and deli
Bus Tours: Yes. Ask about coupon book.
Notes or Attractions: Dollywood amusement park is approximately 3 miles away.

Lenox Factory Outlet
Five Oaks Factory Stores
1645 Parkway

Directions: From I–40, take exit 407 onto Highway 441. Outlet is approximately 7 miles south on the left.
Phone: (615) 428–4745
Hours: *January–March:* 9:00 A.M.–6:00 P.M., Sunday–Thursday; 9:00 A.M.–9:00 P.M., Friday–Saturday. *April–December:* 9:00 A.M.–9:00 P.M., Monday–Saturday; 9:00 A.M.–7:00 P.M., Sunday.
Credit Cards: Discover, MasterCard, Visa
Personal Checks: Yes
Food: A variety of choices in the immediate area
Bus Tours: Yes

No Nonsense & More
Five Oaks Factory Stores
1645 Parkway, Suite C-8

Directions: From I–40, take exit 407 onto Highway 441. Outlet is approximately 7 miles south on the left.
Phone: (615) 428–9194
Hours: *January–March:* 10:00 A.M.–6:00 P.M., Sunday–Thursday; 10:00 A.M.–9:00 P.M., Friday–Saturday. *April–December:* 9:00 A.M.–9:00 P.M., Monday–Saturday; 9:00 A.M.–7:00 P.M., Sunday.
Credit Cards: Discover, MasterCard, Visa
Personal Checks: Yes, with driver's license

Food: Yes, at food court
Bus Tours: Yes. Call the center management for information.
Alternate Transportation: Pigeon Forge Trolley service stops within 4 blocks of center.
Notes or Attractions: Located in the Smoky Mountains tourist area. Near Pigeon Forge, Dollywood, and a host of other major attractions. Many nearby hotels.

Tellico Plains

Duck Head Outlet Store
Route 4—Highway 68

Directions: From Knoxville, take I–75 to Sweetwater. Take Highway 68. Exit north to Madisonville. Go thirty to forty-five minutes, then look for the Duck Head sign on the left. Turn left on Old Highway 68; take the second left at the Tellico High School sign.
Phone: (615) 253–2616
Hours: 9:30 A.M.–5:00 P.M., Monday–Friday; 8:00 A.M.–4:00 P.M., Saturday; closed Sunday
Credit Cards: Discover, MasterCard, Visa
Personal Checks: Yes, with driver's license or picture identification, date of birth, and work phone number
Additional Savings: Two inventory sales, last week of December and last week of June. Sales run constantly with 25 to 50 percent off ticketed prices.
Food: Fast food and deli within half a mile of outlet
Bus Tours: Yes
Notes or Attractions: Outlet located within Cherokee National Forest; near campgrounds, a fish hatchery, and the Bald River Falls; forty minutes north of the Lost Sea in Sweetwater.

Union City

Factory Stores of America
Highway 51

Directions: Located on Highway 51 North
Phone: (901) 885–6465 (Vanity Fair)
Hours: *January–July:* 9:00 A.M.–7:00 P.M., Monday–Thursday; 9:00 A.M.–9:00 P.M., Friday–Saturday; 12:00–6:00 P.M., Sunday. *August–December:* 9:00 A.M.–8:00 P.M., Monday–Thursday; 9:00 A.M.–9:00 P.M., Friday–Saturday; 12:00–6:00 P.M., Sunday.
Outlets:
Bass Shoes
Prestige Fragrance & Cosmetics, PFC Fragrance
Van Heusen
Vanity Fair
Credit Cards: Discover, MasterCard, Visa
Personal Checks: Yes
Food: Fast food in the immediate area
Notes or Attractions: Located twenty-five minutes from Reelfoot Lake and one hour from Kentucky Lake.

Product Index

Reebok, 44
Shoe Store for Less, 47

Shoes, Men's
Allen Edmonds, 2
Athlete's Foot, 3
Bally, 4
Banister Shoes (U.S. Shoe), 4
Bass Shoes, G. H. Bass, 5
Boot Factory, 7
Burlington Shoe, 9
Cole-Haan, 13
Converse Shoe, 13
Dexter Shoes, 16
Diamond Factory & Eelskin Outlet, 16
Famous Footwear, 19
Famous Name Brand Shoes, 19
Florsheim Shoe, 21
Foot Factory, 21
Footprints, 21
Frugal Frank's Shoe Outlet, 22
Gitano, 23
Hush Puppies, 28
JC Penney Catalog Outlet, 29
Johnston & Murphy, 30
Little Red Shoe House (Wolverine), 34
Naturalizer, Etc., 36
Nike, 37
Rack Room Shoes, 43
Reading Shoe, 44
Reebok, 44
Rolane, 45
Shoe Show, 47
Shoe Store for Less, 47
Shoe Strings, 47
Sports Outlet, 48

Shoes, Women's
Allen Edmonds, 2
Athlete's Foot, 3
Bally, 4
Banister Shoes (U.S. Shoe), 4
Barett Shoes, 4
Bass Shoes, G. H. Bass, 5
Brown Shoe Co., 8
Burlington Shoe, 9
Capezio, 10
Cole-Haan, 13
Converse Shoe, 13
Dexter Shoes, 16
Diamond Factory & Eelskin Outlet, 16
Easy Spirit & Co., 17
Etienne Aigner, 19
Famous Footwear, 19
Famous Name Brand Shoes, 19
Foot Factory, 21
Footprints, 21
Frugal Frank's Shoe Outlet, 22
General Shoe Factory to You, 22
Gitano, 23
Hush Puppies, 28
JC Penney Catalog Outlet, 29
J. G. Hook, 30
Joan & David, 30
Little Red Shoe House (Wolverine), 34
Naturalizer, Etc., 36
NCS Shoe, 37
Nickels, 37
Nike, 37
9 West, 38
Rack Room Shoes, 43
Reading Shoe, 44
Reebok, 44

Outlet Index

A & K Gift,
FL: Orlando, 90

Accessorize
FL: Orlando, 89

Accessory Stop
GA: Dalton, 113
SC: Myrtle Beach, 190

Acme Boot
AL: Athens, 58
FL: Davenport, 76
     Daytona Beach, 76
     Ft. Pierce, 79
     Key Largo, 84
     Ocala, 88
     St. Augustine, 95
     Tampa, 100, 101
GA: Lake Park, 124
KY: Bowling Green, 132
     Louisville, 139
     Paducah, 139
TN: Clarksville, 204
     Cookeville, 205
     Dickson, 207
     East Ridge, 207
     Goodlettsville, 208
     Harriman, 208
     Knoxville, 210
     Murfreesboro, 212

Adolfo II
AL: Foley, 66
FL: Ft. Pierce, 79
     Naples, 86
     Orlando, 89
GA: Commerce, 112
NC: Blowing Rock, 157
     Burlington, 158
SC: Hilton Head Island, 187
     Myrtle Beach, 190

Adrienne Vittadini
AL: Foley, 66
TN: Chattanooga, 202

Aileen
AL: Boaz, 59
     Foley, 66
AR: Hot Springs, 72
FL: Ft. Myers, 78
     Ft. Pierce, 79
     Ft. Walton Beach, 81
     Kissimmee, 84
     Naples, 86
     Orlando, 89
     Panama City, 94
     St. Augustine, 96
     South Daytona, 97
     Sunrise, 98
     University Park, 101
     West Palm Beach, 103
GA: Adel, 106

Wolf Camera & Video
FL: Orlando, 89

Yes Brazil
FL: Orlando, 93

Young Generations
FL: Orlando, 89
GA: Dalton, 114
SC: Bluffton, 180
Myrtle Beach, 191
TN: Pigeon Forge, 214

Mall Index

Alpine Village Outlets
GA: Helen, 122

Barefoot Landing
SC: North Myrtle Beach, 193

Belz Factory Outlet Center
FL: Orlando, 88
TN: Pigeon Forge, 214

Boaz Outlet Center
AL: Boaz, 59

Burlington Manufacturers Outlet Center
NC: Burlington, 158

Cannon Village
NC: Kannapolis, 165

Commerce Factory Stores
GA: Commerce, 111

Coral Isle Factory Stores
FL: Naples, 86

Dalton Factory Stores
GA: Dalton, 113

Factory Stores Adel
GA: Adel, 106

Factory Stores of America
FL: Graceville, 82
KY: Georgetown, 135
    Hanson, 137
NC: Smithfield, 172
TN: Union City, 221

Fashion Outlets
AL: Boaz, 61

Foothills Factory Stores
SC: Spartanburg, 196

Hot Springs Factory Outlet Stores
AR: Hot Springs, 72

Jent Factory Outlets
KY: Horse Cave, 137

Lake Park Mill Store Plaza
GA: Lake Park, 124

Low Country Factory Outlet Village
SC: Bluffton, 178

Lumberton Outlet Center
NC: Lumberton, 167

Manufacturer's Outlet Center
FL: Ft. Pierce, 79
    Ft. Walton Beach, 81